BECKETT'S
FRIENDSHIP
1979–1989

For Josette Hayden, and for Bernard Pautrat
In memory of Nicolas Abt (1889–1965)

TO MY SON,
NICHOLAS BERNOLD

BECKETT'S
FRIENDSHIP
1979–1989

André Bernold

Translated by Max McGuinness

Photographs by John Minihan

THE LILLIPUT PRESS
DUBLIN

Originally published in French as
L'Amitié de Beckett 1979–1989
by Hermann Éditeurs, 1992

Published in 2015 by
THE LILLIPUT PRESS
62–63 Sitric Road, Arbour Hill
Dublin 7, Ireland
www.lilliputpress.ie

ISBN 978 1 84351 640 8

10 9 8 7 6 5 4 3 2 1

A CIP record for this title is available
from The British Library.

Set by Marsha Swan in 9.5 pt on 16 pt Clarendon
with Akzidenz Grotesk titling
Printed in Navarre, Spain, by GraphyCems

Preface

MAX McGUINNESS

'A book is the product of another self than the one we display in our habits, in society, and in our vices.' So wrote Marcel Proust in *Contre Sainte-Beuve*, the name given to an unfinished critical essay-cum-novel that constitutes an early version of *À la recherche du temps perdu*. Yet Proust's social self has become so comprehensively identified with his book that the village of Illiers, where he spent summers as a boy, even took the step of officially transforming art into life, rebranding itself as Illiers-Combray in 1971 to mark the centenary of his birth.

This was three years after Roland Barthes published a brief essay proclaiming 'the death of the author', a nostrum that quickly acquired near-axiomatic status for a generation of literary theorists.[1] This was not exactly a new idea: T.S. Eliot had insisted just as forcefully that facts about an author's life were of no direct relevance to our understanding of his work. However, in the wake of 1968 it was invested with a new political fervour as Michel Foucault, in his lecture 'Qu'est-ce qu'un auteur?', vowed an end to the 'author concept' for the sake of the 'free circulation, free manipulation, free composition, decomposition, and recomposition of fiction'.[2]

Samuel Beckett was caught up in this debate from the off. Foucault opens his lecture with a quotation from *Texts for Nothing*: 'What matter who's speaking'. (Ironically, this is attributed to Beckett himself, then at the height of his fame as an author, in the very year when he would be awarded the Nobel Prize, with no mention of the text in which it is found.) The choice can hardly have been accidental. There is probably no other author whose works lend themselves so readily to the kind of criticism Foucault is endorsing, for which expansive polysemy constitutes the guiding principle. And few have resisted the temptation to treat Beckett's work as a literary Rorschach test. *Waiting for Godot* alone has, *inter alia*, been interpreted as an allegory for British colonialism in Ireland, for the author's experiences in the French Resistance, for the Cold War and fear of nuclear holocaust, for the death of God, for the Second Coming, for Hegel's master-slave dialectic, for Freud's structural model of the psyche, for Jung's theory of the self, and for Camus' ideas about the absurdity of existence. A few years ago, I attended a talk following a performance of Peter Brook's production of five short Beckett plays where two respected Beckett scholars immediately disagreed about whether Beckett was an 'existentialist' and the discussion pretty much failed to move on from there.

But at the very point when large sections of the academy resolved to do away with the author, the public became increasingly interested in these allegedly sepulchral figures (though not always in their inconveniently long and difficult books) – Illiers' opportune hyphenation being symptomatic of an emerging global boom in literary tourism. (The local councillors responsible for this name change had perhaps not read as far as *Le Temps retrouvé* where Combray becomes the scene of heavy fighting, unlike their own pleasant little town, which is located over 100 kilometres south-west of Paris and thus remained far from the front line throughout the First World War.) Meanwhile, the love lives, feuds and bank accounts of living authors were regularly transformed into front-page news. Beckett, as André Bernold puts it here, became 'the most watched silhouette on the boulevard Saint-Jacques'.

Not all of this was mere prurience. The latter part of the twentieth century, despite the rise of post-structuralism, was also a golden era for literary biography, which yielded, among others, Richard Ellmann's *James Joyce* and *Oscar Wilde*, Claude Pichois and Jean Ziegler's *Baudelaire*, Norman Sherry's *The Life of Graham Greene*, Graham Robb's *Balzac*, R.F. Foster's *W.B. Yeats: A Life*, and Jean-Yves Tadié's *Marcel Proust*, not forgetting James Knowlson and Anthony Cronin's biographies of Beckett. We thus know infinitely more about these writers than we did fifty or sixty years ago. This can but have an influence on how we approach their works.[3] Despite his deep sense of privacy, Beckett's persona has been so widely written about that it has become unavoidably mixed up in our imagination with what Bernold calls his 'creatures'. Whether or not Barthes and Foucault were right to dismiss the figure of the author, when confronted with Vladimir wincing or Krapp hunched over his tape recorder or Molloy resting on his bicycle, one's mind always seems to turn to the 'gentle mask' placed over the 'severe ossature' immortalized in John Minihan's photographs, surely among the most iconic images of the twentieth century. We simply cannot help it.

This is perhaps less true of other writers, even those whose lives have been similarly well documented. We can appreciate *The Waste Land* without being irresistibly drawn to the prickly man behind it; we can puzzle over 'Pierre Menard, Author of the Quixote' without being entranced by its fastidious creator; Bertolt Brecht's indignities need not intrude upon our enjoyment of *The Threepenny Opera*. But the depth of Beckett's personal kindness and humanity constantly seem to shine through his work.

Bernold records an occasion when Beckett's German translator, Elmar Tophoven, noticed that someone was using a mirror to flash a beam of light into Beckett's apartment. It transpired to be an inmate in neighbouring La Santé Prison who 'was sending a signal to the free man opposite, the nondescript man, who, alone, would make sweeping semaphore gestures in return, which signified nothing save for: "Courage!"' There, in microcosm, is Beckett's perennial feeling of solidarity with the underdog, the intuitive sympathy for the outcast, which left over a thousand convicts in rapt silence during the

1957 production of *Waiting for Godot* inside San Quentin Prison. And it reappears here in the closeness offered to an isolated young man, met randomly on the street, who was 'unequal in everything, besides in affection'. Beckett even used to worry about whether his friend had a warm coat.

As Bernold admits, by themselves, facts about an author's appearance or behaviour do not necessarily offer any particular insight into his writing:

> There was in Beckett's very appearance something like an undefined mute exclamation. Always verticality, the cliff face, the bird. Immersion in silence could become so deep that when one of us reverted to words he would take care to articulate them slowly, as if the other had become deaf. [...] Perhaps this has no relation to this writer, one writer among so many others, that is not purely contingent and assuredly without significance for his work, or interest for anybody, unless linked to this *ponderación misteriosa* is the event of friendship.

Ponderación misteriosa – the entry of God into a work of art, the moment, in other words, where the creator is juxtaposed with his creation. To what effect? What can the creator tell us about his creation that is not already there for all to see?

All friendship can offer is one potential point of entry into the hermeneutic circle. For it is through friendship that otherwise incidental details about a person are invested with meaning. In this way, over ten years of regular meetings, consisting of long silences punctuated with wry remarks, lovingly exchanged quotations and moments of exquisite tenderness, Bernold became increasingly attuned to the centrality of the voice in Beckett's life and later work. 'I have always written for a voice,' he says during one of their meetings. And as the man's physical powers faded, so his language became ever more refined and spare; the voice seems to be investing its final energies in a display of extreme concision before fading out for good. This comes across in the numerous pithy quips, infused with a distinctive Franco-Dublin irony, that peppered their conversations: 'I will be there if they need obscurement'; 'all my life, I've been banging on the same nail'; 'put a bit of order in my confusion'; 'getting down to insomnia'; 'you're looking surgical this morning'. It also emerges in Beckett's rare comments about his work: 'I'll need some substantive-actors,' he tells Bernold, who interprets this curious expression as being suggestive of a parallel between voice and movement in his final plays – each stripped back to its barest, most essential elements. 'The immobile or almost immobile actor,' writes Bernold, 'is like a substantive forgotten in a big unfinished sentence.' Both language and movement here approach a vanishing point – a fantasy of musical purity within nothingness that at once reflects the preoccupations of some of Beckett's juvenilia and the perspective of an old man. 'Things get simpler,' he remarks to Bernold, 'when the horizon shrinks.'

Becoming Beckett's friend entailed challenges similar to those presented by his work. Like the audience members at the first production of *Waiting for Godot*, many, on this evidence, would not have stuck around for the second act:

> A card by return post gave day, time, and place for a meeting. This was the first interview; it lasts exactly one hour in near total silence. I don't remember a single word. We sat opposite each other, royally mute. I believe I remember that we were hunched forward a bit, so as to examine the deep breathing of this silence.

By Bernold's account, their subsequent meetings tended to be only slightly more loquacious. And yet within this silence there emerged flashes of wit and insight, carefully set down by Bernold, and a deep mutual consideration. Long passages of puzzlement, followed by moments of blinding clarity. This is how Beckett's writings often unfold: an abstruse, elliptical build-up suddenly yielding to a rueful punchline, a burst of lyricism or an unforgettable glimpse of pathos – the story of the world and the trousers in *Endgame*, Watt's epiphany about 'the poor old lousy earth', Krapp's 'most ... unshatterable association', the final gesture of supplication and defiance in *Act Without Words II* and *Catastrophe*. (*Beckett's Friendship* itself seems to replicate this pattern.) Of course you cannot have one without the other – penitence before atonement, difficulty before transcendence.

So it is with friendship. After all, friends can often seem like more trouble than they're worth. Unlike romantic or familial attachments, friendship has no obvious *raison d'être*. There is nothing necessary about a friendship; its rituals and codes are fluid and undefined. One could, and many do, live an outwardly successful life without having any real friends at all. Friendship, like literature, is optional. And yet we persevere through boredom, disappointment, embarrassment, irritation, we stick by each other and are perhaps rewarded by a glimpse of the deeper self – the one that Proust said was revealed through literature.

Beckett's Friendship provides us with such a glimpse. And what we see is a man who was, in every respect, as good as his words.

Paris, 2015

NOTES

1. Roland Barthes, 'La Mort de l'auteur', *Manteia*, no. 5, 1968.
2. Michel Foucault, 'Qu'est-ce qu'un auteur?', *Bulletin de la Société française de philosophie*, vol. 64, no. 3, 1969.
3. I heard Edmund White make a version of this point during a round-table discussion at a Proust conference held at Columbia University in October 2013.

NOTE ON THE TEXT: Beckett systematically translated his own works from French into English and vice versa. In most cases, wherever the original text includes a quotation from Beckett in French, this has been replaced by its English equivalent. The English titles of his works have also been used. The exceptions to this are two of his *Mirlitonnades*, which were never translated by him and appear here in the translator's own translation. Unless otherwise stated, all other translations of quotations from works by other authors are the translator's own.

BECKETT'S
FRIENDSHIP
1979-1989

This simplicity, which great men almost alone dare permit themselves and which brings forth, in its contrast, all that is rare about them, was perfect in him.

Fontenelle, *Éloge de Malebranche* (1716)

S amuel Beckett's great beauty drew many glances but it also gave him a kind of invisibility. People in the street, without knowing him, would often notice him but those he encountered frequently and who knew his name would seemingly pay him little attention. The habit of glory, his politeness, his simplicity were not enough to explain this unobtrusiveness, his own and that of others towards him.[1] Rather, it came from his beauty, which was identical in him to his power of self-effacement.

Through memory, we can retrieve this absence as it was within his presence. It allows us to speak of him. 'The closest say only what was close to them, not the distance which asserted itself within this closeness, and the distance ceases with the presence,' writes Maurice Blanchot in *L'Amitié*. But the closeness offered by Samuel Beckett to someone unequal in everything, besides in affection, created a distance of a kind that did not depend on his presence, that inhabited me entirely, and that never ceases. Friendship is mysterious when it is unlikely and without pretence. A glimmer reigns there, faint and without known origin, as distant as when the friends themselves were its source.

Beckett's visible beauty made him someone who was difficult to really see. It hid him, he who did not shield himself. It revealed him through a series of aspects, which were discontinuous and, in the mathematician's sense, discrete. An elliptical creature – that is how he was about himself. The presence of his body, despite his words, was only of use to him intermittently – in the occasional expression on his shifting faces, in the utterances of his different voices, or in his rare gestures and the way he returned to a state of rest. These glimpses of expressivity were so beautiful that they would capture your attention and prevent you from observing what separated them and how they would suddenly disappear, leaving him there with head bowed. In these eclipses, there was nothing you could see or know. It was a matter of accompanying him there. That is where he would remain, between two bursts of light, in a stasis where you had to join him.

His marvellous simplicity came from that static place, from his concern for nothing, from the ease with which he could be nothing, or could often just abandon his powers of concentration and leave them wandering about in front of him on the corner of a table. It was enough to come and sit with him there: you would then feel that the emptiness of the moment – the joyfulness too – and the shifting between grey areas and bright ones were just two aspects of a single attitude that was first apparent from the strange character of his beauty. For it was strange, his beauty. People usually said it was like that of a bird, an eagle. There was a certain vigour to the way he turned or bowed his head, a way of shifting seamlessly from one state to another, which, as much as the famous profile, added to his appearance of being surrounded by space.

The sudden character of our meetings was to be expected, given their perfect punctuality. Often I would come across him in the street, and that is how we first made each other's acquaintance. But when I had the time to see him arriving, his appearance would overtake me. Having barely passed through the door, things would speed up. I would catch sight, in the door frame, of his hand raised high in distant greeting, then, without a beat, came the embrace. My sense of emotion, undimmed these ten years, certainly had something to do with this. But the pace is just that of events in Beckett's texts.

Even before anything had begun, the lulls, the pauses in the emptiness established a rhythm. Perhaps that is what is essential in a meeting – this upbeat, this *jeté battu* before the first note. And what's more, it must be repeated every time. We never failed to do so. It's a matter of tact: *Takt, Auftakt*, as the German has it. This would go on for the first fifteen bars and sometimes even the whole performance. Before uttering a word, with delightful cohesion, our uncertain expressions would strike a series of suspended chords, which slowly detached, one by one, to juxtapose question with answer, bright eyes with teasing mouth, half in jest, half in earnest: 'How are you doing?

– I'm just wondering that myself!' And then *da capo*, the conversation would resume where we had left off a month or two beforehand. (Until his health worsened, there were only three times when we went more than three months without seeing each other.) On occasion we would repeat a good chunk of what we had said.

Sam had several others traits that evoked a bird. Whenever we resumed our silence and Sam was staring at the table without a care, I would look at his forehead and the root of his nose and the roots of his hair. There was a grey cowlick stuck onto his white hair like a crest above the powerful and distinctively creased forehead. His face was just this deeply battered copper pot on which, quite suddenly, two eyes would flick up.

Only with difficulty did I manage to obtain a satisfying mental reading from the map of his wrinkles. I would trace a path through this grid, too complicated to be grasped in a single glance, telling myself that it had just been mapped out. The crumpled might of these lines offered a clue, like figures in the dust (in my opinion, he would not have liked such imagery), to his affinities with rocks and trees. But they lay open across the gentle mask that they placed over the severe ossature. From his knitted brow they rose in parallel arcs above the eye sockets – like unfolded wings – and then fell back towards the cheekbones, disappearing beneath his eyelashes. In this way, his eyes were overhung by the distinctive markings of a sparrow hawk. A few liver spots, clearer on the right side than on the left, or maybe the other way around, softened this majestic appearance with a touch of humbleness.

Above the nose, one noticed the bizarre yet unmistake-able shape of a trigram. The vertical axis was joined by two arms, which formed the outline of a fellow dancing. These shifting lattices made his entire face into a tangled weave that took hold of one's astonished gaze. There followed a generalized wavering of the elements of expressivity and our faces became, all in all, quite hidden. In this way, we had taken to playing games of *foggy physiognomy*, using vagueness like an unprompted thin smile. Heedless of how we might come across, freed from all obligation for mutual exchange, we would admit to having 'nothing to say to each other', and this would reassure us enough so that we were on the whole quite talkative. From time to time, he would look at me with a certain insistence but this never particu-larly disturbed me. I do not know exactly what he thought of my youthfulness. But he picked up on the humours that affected my face and did so precisely enough to be able sometimes to guess what I was thinking.

Birds drew his interest. We had made similar observa-tions about owls and the relationship between their cries and the quantity of light scattered throughout the night: 'Last night, I heard an owl again for the first time in a long while. I used to hear them quite often in Ussy as well as in Paris around the Luxembourg Gardens. Now it's become rare. The owl's cry is so moving. – There is also one of them in Colmar, which cries out when I've got the light on. – They are protesting against the light.' (19 July 1985)

One day (August 1984), back from Ussy, he tells me that a tit has just nested in his letterbox. I can see him now, tracing the form of the nest on the table, ⌐‿⌐ a bowl-shape, 'with a landing strip for the mother, made out of twigs and lined with moss to make it snug. Little inanimate balls of golden brown colour, beaks held open, then the fully formed birds fly off. An incomprehensible marvel.' (Always this perception of discontinuous states.) 'Each body is a momentary spirit, that is to say without recollection ...' I sent him these lines of Leibniz's, one 22 December, in 1983. That same day, I escaped accidental death by a whisker.

I first met Beckett in the street, right in front of my home at the time. I had been in touch with him several years beforehand. I had written to him, when I was very young, from the provinces. He had replied – I believe he almost always used to reply. His first letter bears only one word; my own had not asked for anything more. He had taken me word for word. His own one was 'Yes'.

I began my studies in Strasbourg, sat the entrance exam for the École Normale, moved in there, and immediately set about searching for him, which is to say: wandering around the fourteenth arrondissement. Nothing came of this. One Saturday in November, returning to the rue d'Ulm, I find him standing in front of the railings of number 45. He was looking at the window on the left-hand side of the second floor above the porch. It was the first time in over ten years, he later told me, that he had passed by there. I turn around and start retracing my steps, then I double back again; he was moving away and I follow him a little, without wishing to tail him, and I thus eventually overtake him, whereupon I *can no longer hear him* and slow down without turning around. The twists and turns of traffic wind up leaving us side by side in front of a pedestrian crossing. I ask him to confirm his identity and state my own. I am struck by his Irish accent. Together we move along the length of the street. Beckett was walking on the edge of the pavement, very slowly, and I, in the gutter, adjusted my stride to his own. The comedy of the situation did not escape me, but neither did Beckett's embarrassment. Consequently, I bid him farewell quite abruptly. And that's when an immense smile lights up his face and he holds out his hand whilst saying this to me: 'If you need anything at all, let me know.' Then he goes off. I watch him moving away. I didn't expect to see him ever again. 'Let me know', 'anything at all', this was a friendly way of speaking however, one which would reoccur.

This second encounter, like the first ('Yes'), pleases me not because it happened to me but because it took place in a state of near emptiness, because it remains empty even though it was highly fortuitous. I feel both these things, which suit me perfectly, at the same time. I do not want anything beyond that. Empty, but not pointless. For instead of our trajectories separating for ever, they intersect again a bit further on, at an absolutely singular point, and then the crossing repeats itself. (The pointless meeting and its ineluctable repetition, an obsession in his work, were pitfalls we avoided.)

What happens next? Events begin to move along. Pleasantly, each of us played two modest moves (by correspondence). Nothing suggested that the game was going to change in style. Three months later (time had gone walkabout) I sent Beckett four lines from Malherbe (they were some of the best). What happened then? I don't know. A card by return post gave day, time, and place for a meeting. This was the first interview; it lasts exactly one hour in near total silence. I don't remember a single word. We sat opposite each other, royally mute. I believe I remember that we were hunched forward a bit, so as to examine the deep breathing of this silence.

A lot has been said about Beckett's silences. For me, they were entirely normal. They came from a man who did not have much to add to what he had already expressed in his books. Respecting such habits went without saying. Besides, I shared the same ones myself, for I had nothing to add to nothing. And I didn't have any questions to ask either.

Already we were tinkering with the device that would amplify this bare minimum to its full power. What we required was a system consisting of a small number of fluctuating signals. Such a comfortable silence provided a good foundation. Once this was set down, it became necessary to divide up the available quantity of words. Sam, with his customary generosity, took it upon himself to speak more at first than I did. It would be a pleasant surprise, at our subsequent meetings, just to hear him start off on stories that had been picked up again and finished off over the years as the mood took him. But a kind of balance had to be struck quite quickly, which assumed that this problem would be resolved: what was I going to say to him?

But it was hardly a problem. Humanity supplied a resource.[2] However, it was obviously not a question of making conversation. We did not discuss, other than briefly, practical questions or those relating to technical aporias. So what about keeping each other company? That would have been fine, but of company, he had less need than I, and in friendship things must be equal.

As a result, we did engage in conversation all the same, but in a special way. We would spend our time sending each other signals, both from afar and close at hand. What did we mean by this? A 'signal' was an element of the situation, real or virtual, in which we found ourselves, such that what one of us sent out already included a fragment of what the other would send back in return. A signal was only a 'signal' for our purposes if the way in which it 'launched itself from the background' (the background formed by the relationship between us) included an indication of how to replace it elsewhere within that background. It is a recognizable form of the game, and maybe the principle of all politeness – a reciprocal form since each move is in some way preceded by the next one, anticipated within a feature of the move to be played straight afterwards. One has the sense it was like playing music. And all this also bore a good deal of resemblance to certain parts of his theatrical work.

Such a mode, by its very nature, is difficult to put into examples, as it is inseparable from the whole it expresses. And so this is how we used to go on, each figuring out his game, keeping an eye on the other. A mosaic is what we were creating – a coherent mosaic, an easy puzzle, grey, typically enough, and without a pattern, but where each tile, once set down, would fill two spaces at once.

Sometimes, however, one would remain empty. The plane would disappear, folded straight up, devastatingly snuffed out by a single spark of absence between the momentarily displaced poles as the negative arc of one was stretched over to the other. There was nothing more to be done. We would stay there for a bit longer and then we would part cheerfully, for our boredom was of no importance, not even for him, not even for me; and once back on the street, the whole thing would already be consigned to oblivion.

He had hardly any interest in himself: from this stemmed his elegance. I can still see the strange elegance of his walk – uneven, determined, as if impeded by something. It had an inflexible quality, seemingly wishing, with each step, to double back

> with feet firm
> though waiting no more
> he moves in front of himself
> wandering without fore[.][3]

He would move slowly, with a careful and obstinate slowness, taking little steps, probably busy actually counting them one by one, bolt upright but with eyes cast down, limping very slightly on his left foot, which I felt he only set down with great care, a little crookedly. From this resulted an imperceptible shrug of the shoulder that I saw as his defining feature. Whenever I tried to account for our friendship, I used to imagine that we must have recognized in something analogous to this shrug, but transposed to incorporeal form, a characteristic common to both of us.

I would also readily accept that, among the signals given out, a few of them, decisive and invisible, had escaped from me and reached him without my realizing it. Whence the inalienable character of the obscure background, which was absolutely obvious to me from the off. Several threads detached from his youth were thus drawn across this background – I felt this at once fleetingly and with certainty. They were undone threads, wandering and roaming lines that criss-crossed his existence and came into contact with my own over very short distances. Beckett sometimes seemed to forget the age gap between us and spoke to me as if I had been around at points in time that he would look back on. I was quite touched by this. 'Marcel Duchamp lived on the rue Hallé, you remember?' He recalled his chess games with him – 'he would give me a rook and then he would win!' – and the beauty of his wife. It was with them that Beckett and Suzanne had first taken refuge after the Gestapo raid. He would go on to spend his final days very near there.

We would readily speak about crossing over lines. Recounting the events of the war lent itself to this, as did stories of trips back and forth between France, Ireland, Germany and England. Beckett was not indifferent to the fact that I read a lot of German; he used to read some too, and our conversations on literature reflected this predilection. We would frequently return to the subject of his journeys across Germany at the beginning of the thirties, which still lived on intensely within him. It was from Kassel that he had sent his resignation to Trinity College. To flee, he would recollect, to drop everything in a hurry, leaving it all behind him in a heap (he said it in German: '*Im Stich*'), that had been his attitude at certain times.

Within an equally deep and sheltered layer, I perceived his attachment to Joyce's memory. He spoke to me a lot about him, about his person, about his family and those around him, but he never said anything out of the ordinary about their relationship. The relationship was not figurable. Joyce's personality belonging to the public domain, he would restrict himself to touching up his portrait. One day, curiously, he wondered aloud: 'I wonder when Joyce used to write. Probably at night.' Whenever Joyce telephoned he would leave his number, which the concierge repeated in a southern accent. I still have this voice in my head, Sam would tell me, the voice of the concierge with the southern accent asking me to call back (and he would sing out the number). I hear this voice of a voice, I hold on to this signal of a signal of a signal.

I would make use of foreign languages when writing to Beckett, and sometimes in his presence, so as to attenuate my remarks. What could I give him, he who had tried to lose and who gave me so much? Simulacra, tattered openwork, transparent objects. As if I had said: 'Look, the snow will end up covering everything' (together we sang, *sotto voce*, the first *lied* of *Winter Journey*). Such a gauze I found ready made in the work of the poet Hölderlin, to which Beckett had paid close attention. What is more, I saw them, Hölderlin and Beckett, as being at the extremities of 'modern literature'; I saw Pim as the last avatar of those pure souls who, having walked close to the gods, now find themselves crawling along in the mud:

Denn wo die Reinen wandeln, vernehmlicher
Ist da der Geist, und offen und heiter blühn
Des Lebens dämmernde Gestalten

Da, wo ein sicheres Licht erscheint.

(*'An eine Fürstin von Dessau'*)

For where the pure ones wander, more palpable
Is the shade, and openly and gaily bloom
The crepuscular forms of life
In that place where a sure light appears.

('To a Princess from Dessau')

For his seventy-seventh birthday, on 13 April 1983, in my parcel there was this:

Reif sind, in Feuer getaucht, gekochet,
Die Frücht und auf der Erde geprüfet und ein Gesetz ist,
Dass alles hineingeht, Schlangen gleich,
Prophetisch, träumend auf
Den Hügeln des Himmels. Und vieles
Wie auf den Schultern eine
Last von Scheitern ist
Zu behalten. Aber bös sind
Die Pfade. Nämlich unrecht,
Wie Rosse, gehn die gefangenen
Element und alten
Gesetze der Erd. Und immer
Ins Ungebundene gehet eine Sehnsucht. Vieles aber ist
Zu behalten. Und not die Treue.
Vorwärts aber und Rückwärts wollen wir
Nicht sehn. Uns wiegen lassen, wie
Auf schwankem Kahne der See.

('Mnemosyne', *Dritte Fassung*)

Ripe, immersed in fire, cooked

Are the fruits and on the ground examined and it is
   a law
That everything goes inside, like snakes,
Prophetic, dreaming on
The hills of heaven. And much,
Like on the shoulders
A load of logs,
Is for keeping. But evil are
The paths. Decidedly astray,
Like horses, go the imprisoned
Elements and old
Laws of the earth. And always
Into unravelment goes a flight of nostalgia. But much is
For keeping. And vital, fidelity.
But forwards and backwards we wish
Not to see. Let us roll, as if
Aboard a boat rocking on the sea.

               ('Mnemosyne', third version)

In November of that year I received, along with a poem about the title and some very mordant commentary, a copy of *Disjecta*, a collection of circumstantial texts that had just been published. Among the beautiful and very revealing pieces of juvenilia, there is an extract from his first (unfinished) 'novel', *Dream of Fair to Middling Women* (1932), which includes this strange passage:

> I think now ... of the dehiscing, the dynamic *décousu* of a Rembrandt [...] in all of which canvases during lunch on many a Sunday I have discerned a disfaction, a désuni, an Ungebund, a flottement, a tremblement, a tremor, a

tremolo, a disaggregating, a disintegrating, an efflorescence, a breaking down and multiplication of tissue, the corrosive ground-swell of Art. It is the Pauline *cupio dissolvi* [I wish to be dissolved]. It is Horace's *solvitur acris hiems* [bitter winter melts away]. It might even be at a pinch poor Hölderlin's *alles hineingeht Schlangen gleich*. [everything goes inside like snakes] *Schlangen gleich!*'[4]

I had undoubtedly quoted the *same* text as Beckett had fifty-one years beforehand, at the very moment when his reminiscence of the distant past was, unbeknownst to me, re-emerging into the light of day. It was the final verses, but not only them, which had, I believe, led me to do so; in those lines I saw a prolepsis of the famous passage in *Krapp's Last Tape*: '—upper lake, with the punt [...] We drifted in among the flags and stuck. [...] We lay there without moving. But under us all moved, and moved us, gently, up and down, and from side to side.'[5]

Mnemosyne also seems to dwell in the dream formed in 1932 where she would have encountered, under the sign of unravelling so characteristic of his own syntax, the Pauline desire for dissolution, Horace's discreet rupture, Rembrandt's triumphant defeat as well as Krapp's own – sadder – of which she would have premonitorily dreamt. ('Krapp, that poor fellow' [21 October 1983]) For it is indeed Memory that emerges from the spools that he listens to repeatedly, where Beckett, in 1958, had recorded a brief confession, which would seem to be like his memorial: '[...] until that memorable night in March, at the end of the jetty, in the howling wind, never to be forgotten, when suddenly I saw the whole thing. The vision at last. [...] – unshatterable association until my dissolution of storm and night with the light of the understanding and the fire [...] We lay there without moving.'[6]

Jacob Burckhardt used to say of Meister Eckhart: 'No dialectical development, but explosions.'[7] It was in analogous fashion that Beckett characterized *Krapp's Last Tape*: 'explosions followed by silences' (7 September 1986). One can say the same of his later plays in their entirety and consider how these explosions succeed each other, disperse, and form a constellation. *Krapp's Last Tape* is a primer, something explodes there whose echoes reverberate: a ceaselessly refigured separation, a visibly irreducible gap, a split, a secession of speech. *Krapp's Last Tape* dramatizes an incurable memory, but which is separated from itself by the voice itself; the radio, a medium adopted by Beckett shortly afterwards, functions like a sieve that separates itself from itself to make pure sensation resonate – a prism for the diffraction of simultaneous voices that are no longer together. This is Beckett's haunting obsession: being together-separate (whether that applies to one or many), of which the most explicit image remains that found in *Play* (1962–3) – a truly infernal obsession. After *Godot*, it dominates his whole œuvre, taking on ever new forms, at times disconcerting in their perfection seemingly arisen from nothing (*Imagination Dead Imagine*, 1965), and yet each is in fact derived from the other (the whole cycle stemming from *The Lost Ones*), possessing an ingeniousness and luxuriance – surprising amid the asceticism of the means, which are not dissimilar to those used by Dante. (But within all this there is a little-noticed case of thematic reversal, of reversion to an earlier motif; for, overall, the problem facing Murphy, Watt, Molloy, Malone, of Mercier and Camier, of Didi and Gogo, and even of the Unnameable is, in certain respects, to leave; but then how it is: always infinitely unleft. It's the problem itself, the problematical in itself, that has moved into the foreground.)

Meanwhile, at the height of summer, Beckett quoted from memory (albeit quite altered, though he didn't realize this) Horace's *solvitur* regarding someone he had liked a lot in his youth; he still associated it with his memory of this person but without knowing why; the following day, in abbreviated form, on the back of a letter, he asked me to track down this verse:

> '*Solvitur acris hiems grata vice*
> *Veris et Favoni*
> (Book 1, Ode IV),'[8]

I responded on the back of a Flemish winter landscape. This back-and-forth had begun in the spring, with him sending the typescript of *What Where* (printed in July), which concludes with these words:

> Good.
> I am alone.
> In the present as were I still.
> It is winter.
> Without journey.
> Time passes.
> That is all.
> Make sense who may.
> I switch off.[9]

Concerning *What Where*, Beckett said on 25 March 1983: 'I sent off the play [to Graz, for the festival for which it was originally intended]; I had a lot of trouble letting it go, I'm not happy with it, I told them to reject it if they don't like it, that I wouldn't be cross. It's a story I've been stuck with for a long time, I just got rid of it like that. I understand nothing about it.' Then on 13 May 1983: 'It's an old story that I don't understand. I wondered what *Where* means. Maybe: where's the way out? The old story of the way out ...' (the sentence trails off in an indistinct murmur). We must take these comments seriously: 'I understand nothing about it ...', 'I wondered what *Where* means ...' – Beckett's solidarity with the conditions that define the problem ...

Here is how he related, on 19 July 1985, the enactment of this 'sinister story'; conceived for the stage, it was adapted for the screen in his presence, in Stuttgart, at the Süddeutscher Rundfunk, from 18 to 28 June 1985. For once, I transcribe a piece of conversation:

'It went very well. I was happy with the work. Very difficult. I set out with a lot of ideas in mind ... idiotic ones ... that it was necessary to abandon. The story of the colours based on Rimbaud ... and the drum rolls [Bam, Bem, etc. are vowels; each was supposed to wear its Rimbaldian colour and appear at the sound of a drumbeat, like the ghosts of *Quad*]. We got rid of all the ornaments. We simplified day after day. As the work went on, we understood everything we didn't need. So: no headdresses, no hair either, no clothes. Just the face. It was technically very difficult. There was one camera per character. The main problem was magnificently resolved by Jim [Lewis]. The main problem was the representation of *Voice*,[10] *Stimme*. Jim came up with the solution of using a most particular image, that of Bam reflected in a mirror ...

—A bit distorting?

—That's it, a bit distorting. That image is present throughout the whole play, along with the different characters on stage at any given point. It was very difficult for the actors. They had to stay still for hours at a time. I don't like insisting on that, but it was necessary. Standing up, still. They had a headrest. The four actors were physically quite different, but made to look the same thanks to some excellent make-up.

—Did they complain?

—No, not at all. They would stay still for around fifty minutes, without doing anything, to allow some adjustments to be made. Fifty minutes of preparation for a few minutes of filming ... The whole thing lasts twelve minutes. It's the result of ten days' work, at the rate of around seven hours per day, from nine to five, with a break. All the interruptions, the corrections made by V [Voice] were abandoned.

The face of Voice, Bam's face reflected in the mirror, lit up the whole time, is motionless, eyes closed. He only has one gesture: when he is alone, at the end, he lowers his head.

V, Bam's voice, is recorded ... the problem of the difference between V and the voice of Bam himself. During the interrogations, the voice had a slight intonation [examples].

V is a white voice, very difficult to find.

—When, during the first interrogation, Bam interrogates Bom (*He didn't say anything ?*), who is this *he*?

—It's he who does not appear. He is dead, *erledigt*. It's the fifth vowel, Bum. It's a sinister story ...

Es ist Winter
Ohne Reise ... [he recites].

There is a great big park in Stuttgart – magnificent – with squirrels who would eat out of your hand. I walked a great deal.'

'I put out' ... Putting out, fading out – the prerogative of the voice, at the end of a sequence, which it alone, guided by gestures, could initiate. Ritual gestures used to accompany our interviews. 'It is the month of May ... for me. Correct. I open.'[11] That's how it used to go, we would arrive, we would play the overture, which was in fact the whole movement; even when we came to the variations and the coda, it was still the overture and already we would be going on our way. Within these passages there reigned a certain brusqueness in the part writing. But everything would be attuned to their reciprocal consonance, in accordance with the key appropriate to making the times dissimulate themselves. A certain boldness in the sequence of the movements – the roughness of cut cloth and the lustre of a pair of scissors lighten the bodies themselves, reduce them to their angles. Friends are light vocal mobiles.

A certain angularity, a measure of the openness and vacuity achieved, used to affect Beckett in his gestures and consequently me in mine. We were courteously abrupt. Courtesy is a sieve and consists in letting nothing get lost that could be abolished with a gesture, by mutual and tacit agreement. Even in his civvies (as he used to say of one actor when he was off-stage, namely David Warrilow who served him marvellously well and whose elegance Beckett admired), Beckett, man of the theatre, remained on the lookout for the possibilities to be gained from his habit of refusing almost everything that came to mind. Leaning on his elbows, smoking in silence, and raising his eyes every now and then to see if the solution was on the horizon, insouciant of scattering ash onto the marble table, his cup of coffee, and the burn-mark-pocked sleeves of his inevitable brown jacket, scrawling on the back of the packet of cigars, going over and over the sketch or the diagram, rising up, through a supple movement of the head that contrasted with the immobility of the body, and plunging back down – that is how he was when he was setting out a problem.

Beckett rarely got annoyed. Disapproval was something he hardly ever put into words, it made him tense up his whole body. Anger would etch a pout of extreme disappointment across his face. Then he would turn away. No one was quicker to disappear before having left. Irony and kindness dominated within him. He proved Beethoven's saying: 'I recognize no sign of superiority other than kindness.' My quotations used to delimit, around this kindness, a stable space. Some coincidences continued to occur within it. The day itself was the perfect example. The calendar would wind on and, thin as a thread, traverse the years intact, weaving together the moments we spent in each other's company; on it would be inscribed friendly names, the cogs of correspondence, a gesture, a piece of clothing, a recurrent intonation, nocturnal dreams. His were composed only of images, he used to say: 'Oh, there are no words, there are only images, a lot of images ...' (12 October 1986). I told him about some of my own: the one where I met Marie, who had just put an end to her days; on a featureless, deserted beach, lying down amid some little flags planted in the sand, she would say to me: 'You see, it's not so terrible.' Or this other one: I would find myself in front of a bridge shrouded in fog, probably collapsed in its middle, and *if I managed to cross it, the world was going to end*. 'May the Lord hear you!' said Beckett. He is there in full, albeit strangely neutral, for his sharpest features did not fall away, but were stretched like a veil, a sail unfurled for death, and were cast off and reabsorbed by the deep, against a rocky jetty between the waters, indivisible and immoveable. That is where gusts and the heave would get mixed up in the enumeration of raw states, states of monotony. Beckett was interested in permanent states that change abruptly, as if he had been able to stretch out there, immobile, and change with them. That, I think, is why he loved music, theatre.

In 1985 I copied out, once again for his birthday, this famous passage of Descartes' on the slightly cross-eyed little girl (letter to Chanut, 6 June 1647) – who, I soon learned from Beckett, for this had escaped me, had been given shelter by him in his first poem (1930: 'I knew this story, I included it in *Whoroscope*; I imagined Descartes used to play hide-and-seek with this little girl [As a child he played with a little cross-eyed girl].[12] I was reading Descartes a lot at the time and this poem is the sad result'):

> For example, when I was a child, I loved a girl of my age who was a bit cross-eyed; consequently, the impression created in my brain by this image, when I looked at her wild eyes, was so bound up with the one that served to stir the feeling of love that, for a long time afterwards, whenever I

saw cross-eyed persons, I would feel more inclined to love them than to love any others [...]

Here all is in the balance, the little girl hesitates, like her eyes. She moves forward, trembling, vacillates, exists no more:

> [...] whenever I saw cross-eyed persons, I would feel more inclined to love them than to love any others, just because they had this flaw; and I was nonetheless unaware that it was because of this. By contrast, ever since I thought about it and recognized that it was a defect, I have ceased to be moved by it.[13]

The useless offering, the overturned table, the journey made for nothing, all this seemed rightly entrusted to Beckett's care, to his gentleness, to his thorough-going kindness.

Sartre attributes to the artist what he calls a degree of inclination over the world. Friendship too inclines over the world at a certain angle. We were poring over the case of the case ('There are no more cases,' Jean Cavaillès reputedly said[14]), leaning on the table with our elbows like on the edge of a dried-up well and speaking in low voices, amid Japanese, German, and Australian businessmen, in the café of the international hotel whose total transformation coincided with Beckett's hospitalization. 'There's no question of returning there, we'll have to find another one,' he said over the telephone. We did not return there, we did not look for another one, there was nothing left but the telephone, then definitive silence.

In this rather chic place where he had been a regular for a long time, he was left in peace without being anonymous. I can see Sam, two days after the death of Roger Blin, sitting there, head in hands, lost in sorrow and deafened by elevator music. I got up to ask for mercy but he held me by the sleeve: 'No, it's no big deal, leave it ...' One would penetrate unnoticed into the lobby of the hotel where groups of people would be waiting around, and from there, up two steps into the café, longer than it was wide, and all in all quite dark in spite of the fine glazed terrace where Beckett hardly ever ventured, preferring to sit facing the wall underneath the clock at the back of the room. It was dominated by dark crimson, brown, and the white of the marble tabletops, veined, cold, sonorous, on which we placed our hands. Beckett would take the chair, leaving me the banquette, which would not have been my first choice. Out of the corner of my eye, I would watch people passing by, mindful of their tiredness. Sometimes I would point them out to him; he would respond with a murmur. I remember the shadow of an old man, preceded by his fingers, feeling the emptiness.

We would contemplate, each man for himself, the nuances of ordinary finitude. There lay dehiscence, defeat, and unravelling. That is where it was necessary to gather up the scattered threads and to calm the trembling, with patched mesh, with delicacy. Avoiding dislocation is at the heart of any encounter. The intention that brought you to me can collapse the moment I come to you. The spindle can break and the skein become tangled up. Yes, I do want to be there, yes, I wanted to speak to you, but look at how tired I suddenly am. Friendship: a hesitant surgeon, a puppeteer with uncertain hands.

To ward off fatigue, the function of friendship must be expressed with a certain precision. Punctuality offered a good place to start. Expressive by itself, being on time was more than a sign of good will, it gave the theme of the fugue of vagueness. It was indeed the least one could do, and maybe there was nothing else. Precision could then extend to everything, distinctly, that very instant, *and come into its own*. This did not involve any mania or obsession so much as a familiar practice of reconnaissance. No code, but transposed notches of love for the monotony of the woods. One day, Beckett said a few unforgettable words about forests, yet they were not even real, certain characters would simply walk there without ever leaving. Here he was proposing a model, the very one in the middle of which we had appeared. Outside, we would glance, between the fences, at some interminable building works that, without bitterness, we called mad.

My sudden inaptitude for orienting myself in space and the loss of the sense of the third dimension I would temporarily feel underlined how much the idea of which direction to take had lost all interest for me. We would swap our spectacles, an idiotic idea of mine that had become one of our rituals, and clown around for a few moments. We also knew how to mumble and make ourselves inaudible. It can never be said enough quite how superfluous intentions are. At an age that is all about saying what you are going to do, I was happy to opt out so completely. The peacefulness of moving away from sharp angles, the peacefulness of the nebulous, the peacefulness of moments when all purpose disappears – everything is evenness there, everything rings with the dullness of wood; whereas in the wavering, indifferent, insignificant attention to oneself, in the possibly violent hurly-burly that is the epitome of rectitude, all faces turn towards the same empty space.

But why, all in all, did he used to see so many people? He would say that he was swamped, beset on all sides, and yet he would keep up his end. It was not to talk of course, as would have been flattering to believe. Rather, it was to go on observing what it is to 'meet' these others, who do not exist, who have never annoyed anyone, to go on confirming that this might not be in vain, inside those interminable forests where everyone is walking around. From this point of view, his friendships prolonged his work, two aspects of which still interested him: that he be delivered from it for ever and yet that he go on: 'All my life, I've been banging on the same nail,' he used to say. Along with the rest of us, the others, he must have been touching the wall; he did not tire of it any more than we did. Why not? Something there persisted in showing its face, which seemed to him worth the trouble of examining from an angle as unencumbered as the space he inhabited: 'I keep nothing' (1981); 'I have nothing, I have nothing' (October 1985). Whatever he said of a personal nature always had a great simplicity, for example: 'Things get simpler when the horizon shrinks.' When he looked back, he would see the lines that had borne him thus far come apart, saying, in a single breath, of the time when he wrote *Texts for Nothing*: 'There was much distress.'

His exactitude offered a glimpse of that state of fixed trembling he had reached, that state of beautiful emptiness, which he expressed through his hands. By virtue of the finished work as much – on a different note – as by the style of his affections, his exactitude took on the strange function of passing into itself, of vanishing, of disappearing into concentration (imagine cubes of salt *dissolving* into cubes of salt), which produced a kind of white all around. One was strongly tempted to bring him armfuls of all that one had encountered en route, to feed this desertic zone, which was black or white depending on whether one looked at him sitting in the light or in the darkness. 'I will be there if they need obscurement,' he once said of a proposal to remake *Film*. Sometimes he would prompt an account of the merest circumstances: 'Did you come on foot?' (of course), and one would say that one had just glimpsed this and that, but it was better to leave things as they were, as if simply breathing them in. One would thus be part of an image quite close to those he put on stage: a cone of light, a patch of gravel, etc. But he would have hated to hear it mentioned.

The possibility, however, of *uncovering I do not know what clue* along the way held a certain importance. Was he inclined to turn aside towards that? No of course, he was waiting for nothing, in spite of his appearance, but his exactitude, making itself expressive, would introduce little cubes of permutable duration. Gestures of arrival, of departure, of accompaniment established the basic sequence, in which would be inserted a mixed sequence: arrival-departure (resumption at arrival of the forms of the preceding farewell), departure-arrival (subtle projection of the next meeting, achieved in part through a strange smile), arrival-accompaniment (or prolongation), accompaniment-departure (or anticipation). The elements 'arrival' and 'departure', as well as all their combinations, were real gestures, but lightened, as if made of parallel characteristics of variable inclination. In him, it was the finely hatched demeanour that accounted for the greater part of his gentleness. A marvellous friend, who would have dismissed such bizarre vocabulary with a long, silent laugh. But such are the values that friendship attained through gestures.

'Arrival', within this schema, concerned the hand, 'departure' was about the movement of the head, hand raised, head inclined. But arrival and departure in turn presented variants that consisted in gaps in the overall duration, the whole of the variations being comparable, moreover, to what are known in mineralogy as inclusions. How do inclusions arrange themselves in a crystal, how are they oriented? We had no direction, but we did set out orientations. (This was curiously related, in my mind, to the existence of unreadable books.) But arrival and departure, once anticipated and divided within themselves, would introduce, accompany and conclude new pastimes. Being early, for example, ever so slightly, by barely a minute or two ahead of the agreed time, which was always rigorously observed down to the very second by at least one of us, that was a pleasure we tacitly accorded one another, taking turns, but I availed of it more often for the satisfaction of seeing him arrive from side-on, looking neither to the right, nor to the left, only beginning to look around after passing a certain spot; slowly following that unchanging course that brought him down the boulevard Saint-Jacques along the wall of the metro line, he would then turn beneath the vault of the bridge that this line crosses, and suddenly appear in front of the café whose windows would momentarily reflect his silhouette, similar to the one I had cut out of the second volume of Geulincx for him and which he had loved and made his own:

Vacillat mens nostra, et ubique titubat,
Et tantum constans in levitate sua est,[15]

a brown shadow sometimes clutching a few letters, or a brown reticule, or a plastic bag, or with an olive canvas musette (US army surplus or imitation thereof) slung over his shoulder, a succession of bags in which there was generally nothing, or at most a pencil and a sheet of paper, a few handkerchiefs of the same substance, the cigars he used to offer me, and from time to time, a copy of the 'latest abortion', as he would happen to call such and such a book of his, only to draw attention straightaway, if it were appropriate, to the quality of the printing. Arriving early merited another overture, made possible a few exclamations, and above all allowed one to familiarize oneself once again with the table. Starting off with a *tabula rasa*, you only really appreciate it all in a busy café, when waiting for a friend (who will definitely come) or for your beloved (who may not).

The entry thus sustained the ellipsis, and the exit, the suspension. But the accompaniment, which variants could it present? That of a mute question: what remains to be expressed without sentences? Let's take it up again, take it up again there, take what up again? The question, said Sam one day, that is in the response. 'For in the response, there is also a question,' he had said quite forthrightly. This most

31

simple sentence particularly pleases me because of the word 'also'. He himself had such preferences – minimal, precise; in this way, he told me he particularly liked the Leopardi quotation, which adorns his essay on Proust and which sometimes, in his old age, returned to his lips: '*In noi di cari inganni, non che la speme, il desiderio è spento*'; the two words '*non che*', those two appeared to him to be the most beautiful. 'Within us dear illusions, it is not even hope, it is desire that is extinguished.' It is not quite that. It is not even that. It is not that at all. '*Non che*' – an expression that transmits. There it is, its face revealed. An expression that changes. It is a *clinamen*. A certain pessimism, of the liveliest kind, essentially allied to humour, comes into contact with the swerve, composes an art of the swerve. In this way the response to the dream, inept or redundant, that, under certain conditions, the world was going to end, is characteristic of a styling line swerving towards its lightest fall. One sees all that irony denies itself (humour), at the point when it sends its object through the depths, along the comfortable reefs of the excluded middle. The swerve is the transition to the excluded middle, the 'resistance to two great temptations, that of the real and that of the lie' (*Henri Hayden*, June 1960).

What was an obvious fact for the reader lingered on in its obviousness for the friend. It rallied everything around: forgotten books, thrown overboard so to speak, global and daily events, habitus, hair and flesh, *sich zusammenfassen*, as the German verb puts it so well – pull yourself together, get a grip, 'put a bit of order in my confusion' as Sam, ever modest, used to say for his part.

And the inflections of Beckett's voice would fade away in turn. Easily perceptible in their minimal variations, they were, however, difficult to remember because they would evolve in extension; tremulous, palpable, they would suddenly move away, enveloped in space; and the air by which one felt the voice was supported, when it would waver for a moment, became rarefied while passing through scattered fields, so that it would end up folding into itself. Rare are voices with a fixed range. Yet I always hear others' better than his, as if, through its murmur, it had overweighted itself so as to better sink into peacefulness. Then it starts to quiver again, limpid with irony, barely more muffled today than when he himself would bring a swift halt to the brief avalanche.

His gaze also used to *open up spaces*: I remember his voice the least badly when I think back to his eyes, which would catch up with the word, abruptly overcome in mid flight, and prolong its vibration, attesting, by their fixedness, the solitude of every vision, albeit retrieved from the depths, released, and free to disappear in the silence. All that is very abstract and would have had made him grumpily shake his head; yet, even stripped of meaning, that is how it is. That is what remains for me hung on the nail stuck in Leopardi's sentence, a display of style transmitted by the inflection of a voice, audible at this singular point.

In the response, a question: he made this remark about an essay of mine that had been inspired by Beethoven's *Notebooks*, which record conversations where, of two voices, only one has been written down. I hadn't really succeeded at this; the idea, and the way he took interest in it, probably came from the fact that he himself had mentioned, six months previously (August 1981), an abandoned attempt at a little play about Beethoven once he had become deaf. This idea consisted in simply making heard the absence of a voice. But what happens if the user of the notebook, say B. (whose deafness is muteness from our point of view), grasps the questions which C. asks faster than C. formulates them? Beckett had foreseen the objection. B.'s advantage over C. was not a source of difficulty; rather that is where the conversation would reach its end. The problem consisted in conveying C.'s disposition through B. – C.'s questions being only written down – or, for that matter, the continual variations of a dialogue broken off in advance. Beckett briefly gave me two pieces of advice: firstly, to write out the dialogue in its entirety and then erase half of it afterwards; secondly, to be very attentive to the positions adopted by the interlocutors in relation to each other within the space.

We left it at that, so as to speak of other things, of *Effi Briest* again (11 February 1982) and, while he was struggling to translate *A Piece of Monologue (Solo)*, of a new project he had conceived in the style of *Quadrat*, 'for two ghosts and voices, in parallel with each other, and restless'. He had not, he said, resolved the question of notation. He lingered for a while over a sketch where he was counting out paces, and which he then handed to me with the cigars. How I would look at him when he was becoming absorbed in an idea like that! So then, this was the man who had strung together the sentences of *The Unnameable*. The same one? Unassuming, turned away, as if abraded to my level. I understood that there are no contemporaries; that greatness, like the shadows, does not let itself be embraced.

I had recognized, in the recorded voices of Georges Bataille and of Pasolini, heard by chance years apart, a gentleness analogous to that of his own, as if a certain inflexibility in the contemplation of disaster was being smothered in his voice. He did not seem to be interested in either man and had forgotten about the existence of the fine article in which Bataille had been among the first to praise *Molloy*. His estrangement from the wish to form judgements led him to retain unexpected details. Of Adorno, about whom I often thought (wondering how he would have appreciated the late works), Beckett used to state, for example, that he had been assassinated by his students. He enjoyed reminiscing about him, though he would not have been convinced by his essay on *Endgame* (*Versuch, das Endspiel zu verstehen*). But he would freely repeat what Adorno had supposedly said to him one evening in the Marquesas Islands, that 'the reception accorded to my work derives from a misunderstanding. – That's sort of my opinion,' Beckett would say and his gaze would take on an inquiring quality.

Perhaps he would often adopt that same gaze, I did not know how deeply, when fixedly scrutinizing a question inaccessible to examination. Failure remained a possibility for him. He would have preferred it, he told me bluntly. But it was magnanimous failure, I believe, that he had in mind, discreet and sumptuously human in the Irish way: like that of John Butler Years, the painter,[16] father of the poet and of Jack B. Yeats (himself a painter with whom Sam had been friendly); his eyes would shine with admiration when he said of him: 'He never used to finish anything! His career was a failure! What we call failure!'

What used to make him exult about John B. Yeats (did he not stir feelings comparable to those that Joyce harboured towards his own father?) was the munificence of the talker squandering his wit all over the place and being paid in return with universal affection: 'He was sought after everywhere for his conversation. He could talk about everything. He finished his days in a little family boarding house in New York; miserable, but surrounded by the admiration of all' (30 November 1986, 15 February 1987).

Listening to him, it seemed that worries about injuring his sombre sincerity or his imponderable susceptibility had to balance out. He rejected fame, but hesitated slightly over Adorno's opinion. Pout and smile: any concessions he might make remained invisible. In the shadow of the background where I dwelt with him, I knew clearly that I would never go forth only wearing such invisible colours, having decided for my part to erase any chance of separating out the basic tones.

What remains to be expressed without sentences? Probably variations of tones, which, in turn, envelop figures, a ring of figures. The tones are turns. The tones are affected by a curvature in the vicinity of the following tone, even if it is still far away. It is the continual overlapping of curves that makes sentences. A sentence can thus be a lot longer than what we normally mean by 'sentence'. Reciprocally, the tones in themselves are extremely brief, only the impetus they communicate keeps spreading out. This is why a Beckett sentence is in reality difficult to quote whether it comes from a text or from his voice. In this respect, in a negative sense, there was a perfect continuity between what he wrote and what he said. Just as, he once said (to summarize) (24 April 1981), 'my texts keep cancelling themselves out', so his speech would disappear into squalls, carried along by brief gusts as if snatched away by a non-existent wind even at the calmest moments. This wind became real the last times I saw him, the wind was carrying off our words for good and we had to raise our voices; Sam would say he had difficulty speaking, turning his head to the side so as not to run out of breath, hands covered with haematoma clenched on his musette. It seemed to me that inside him everything was shifting in a landslide: speech, silence, and difficulties. 'There is a great alp of sand, one hundred metres high, between the pines and the ocean, and there in the warm moonless night, when no one is looking, no one listening, in tiny packets of two or three millions the grains slip, all together, a little slip of one or two lines maybe, and then stop, all together, not one missing, and that is all, that is all for that night, and perhaps for ever that is all [...].'[17] Inaudible, yet figurable shifts. For if the tones change direction depending on the vicinity, they are also curved, in general, around a figure that they inspire but whose own breath passes like a voice through the lattice of this modulated mask. Yes, the tone is also a grille, *Sprachgitter*. (Beckett would say: 'Celan is over my head', and one day when we were all together he asked Elmar Tophoven whether Celan showed his distress in person.) The figures inhabiting the tone can give rise to an image that the voice delegates to speech; the images are given, but the figures only emerge slowly and then move suddenly into sight.

*Samuel Beckett at Le Petit Café, boulevard St-Jacques,
on the ground floor of the PLM Hotel. December 1985, Paris.
This was the écrivain's favourite rendezvous later in life, when he
became too famous to go to other well-known cafés. (John Minihan)*

It is rare that there corresponds to a figure one and only one image; a figure requires a lot of images that are 'parallel' to it. However, an image can occasionally include more than one figure, crystallized in macle; this too is rare, reflecting another kind of rareness familiar to Beckett's writing. Generally speaking, there are effectively more images and fewer tones than there are figures. With Beckett, it is the opposite: each figure is that of a tone although there are empty tones, modulations without voice. But there are more figures than images, not in a numerical sense, but in power of intensity or in capacity for endurance, and straightaway the images are unstable, labile, and susceptible to dissolution.

In conversation with Beckett, the figures would convey subtle appearances. They would usually inhabit his gestures, all the more surely animated for being so minimal. His hands here played a first-order role, knowing how to go through the looking glass, everywhere tracing out, in the air, on the table, with the ash, the networks of the final plan, when hands close together on a hand (*Nacht und Träume*).

On his face, itself a figure that was nearly finished off, the eyes could open up, watchful at the back, the eyes deep down inside,[18] wakefully shut and suddenly agape in the very pale blue of the iris, glimpsed through translucidity, the eyes behind the eyes, immobile.

Very late in the season of our elliptical friendship, I showed him a beautiful phantom quartz crystal ('A needle of crystal inhabited by its own effigy is known as phantom quartz' Roger Caillois); he examined it carefully and asked me what it was to me: 'Like a friend,' I said to him. 'Yes, a friend,' he murmured.

A sense of epiphany, stirring in that limpid gaze, would accompany a kind of interruption, different from those that used to leave many of our remarks hanging in the air. A threshold was crossed without there necessarily having been any passing over. Sentences would emerge, murmured, enunciated, detached. For Danielle Collobert, there was this homage: 'A running jump in all its splendour' (26 November 1983). Or else: 'I had a great stroke of luck, an incomprehensible stroke of luck' (31 August 1981); or else: 'You are very strange.' Or indeed: 'There is still a world to discover' (12 November 1981). Those are some notes of the first tone, the horizontal one.

A low register could descend upon a wild exclamation that it was no use. The vertical tone was suited to other applications and could also be called 'retractile'. And the oblique, the tilted tone, hovered over all the rest, over sentences that passed by, having only a tenuous connection between them – Luther's words in front of the Diet of Worms, which I liked to repeat to him over and over again, a quotation from *Effi Briest* that would come back to him, and several others whose classicism took on an odd form in his silent laughter (according to Milton, I reminded him, angels do not laugh, they only smile; 'So what,' he responded while laughing, 'they are laughing *behind our backs*.')

We were beginning to figure out how to do without sentences. In any event, by the time I met him, any disclosure had long since ceased to serve a purpose. But retrospectively I would recognize, in *How It Is* or *Endgame*, for example, the shards still stuck there, the notch of the inflections his voice could take on, whether it made them audible or left them silent: I don't cling onto this; then it passes; all that, all that, etc. When Nagg, in *Endgame*, takes up the story of the world and the trousers, regarding the voice of the tailor, which Nagg adopts after that of the 'raconteur', Beckett would have wanted the spectator to see, within and through the voice, the figure of the tailor himself, crouching. That is how he intended this voice: crouching, and not otherwise. Once, and only once, he quoted himself to make me hear how his 'personal bugle' sounded. He recited a few words from Clov's exit, really very slowly, his tongue slightly ill at ease on the sibilants: 'They said to me, That's love, yes, yes, not a doubt, now you see how [...] How easy it is. They said to me, That's friendship, yes, yes, no question, you've found it.'[19]

November 1981: the accumulation of trust allowed the left hand to sneak in some facetious themes. Affection always mixed up with irony: 'What are you thinking about? You don't even know yourself!' he chided me one day. A lively sense of mischief often flickered in the big eyes that stared at me from afar; elsewhere, at a slower pace, the lips were moving. He sometimes had what seemed like two faces placed on top of each other: the hollowed-out look, emerging into extension, horizontal, onto which speech, delivered with difficulty in a very low tone, would affix a grill. Thus when he mimed out *Nacht und Träume* (5 July 1982), a short play inspired by one of Schubert's *lieder*,[20] which he had just finished, playing all the roles, the man who dreams, head resting on his hands, the same one dreaming that he is being comforted, his hand raised, the hand that comes down to join his own ... and accompanying himself with the melody that implores the return of these benevolent gestures, with just the words that were necessary, the final ones:

> *Heil'ge Nacht, du sinkest nieder;*
> *Nieder wallen auch die Träume,*
> *Wie dein Mondlicht durch Räume,*
> *Durch der Menschen stille Brust.*
> *Die belauschen sie mit Lust;*
> *Rufen, wenn der Tag erwacht:*
> *Kehre wieder, heil'ge Nacht!*
> *Holde Träume, kehret wieder!*[21]

I was more moved by these hands, Beckett's own, and by this murmured singing than by the play, when I saw it performed. I had the feeling that there, in this mute and invisible scene, the gaze staring at me, and the sense of expectation wherein the imagined thing included us, was the last word of friendship. Memories came flooding back. 'It's morning, evening of the night,'[22] I had read, and then:

> Night who make so many
> Implore the dawn
> Night from grace
> Falls.[23]

Sam used to approach the night with a book before, he would say, 'getting down to insomnia' ('night is becoming an obsession' 13 September 1987) and he would quote Jules Renard: 'meagre broken sleep'.

In any case, he seemed to me to discern strange similarities in the attraction that pantomime exerts over certain major works: those of Artaud, Céline, Genet, as far back as Kafka (the ping-pong balls) and even Kleist.[24] In Beckett's work, it came to light as early as *Act Without Words I* (1957) and *Come and Go* (1966), and then gave rise to original experiments with ... *but the clouds* (1977), *Quadrat I + II (Quad)* (1982), *Nacht und Träume* (1982), and the first version of *What Where* (1983). I see a brilliant modification of this in *Not I* (1973) where it becomes labial. A pantomime of the two lips, nothing but the lips of a mouth, altogether more astonishing than a whimsical dancer or marine invertebrate.

Perhaps, with Beckett, this is a testament to the extreme attention paid to what is so cruelly exposed about life's most wretched traces, the most humble spurts of insignificance when subjected to the crushing forces that their misery vainly hoped to disarm. It is in pantomime that the impossibility of all redemption bursts forth; *Nacht und Träume* is the exception ...

After plotting out in the adjacent space what Jim Lewis and the Süddeutscher Rundfunk were going to surround in penumbra – not quite straightaway, I am no longer exactly sure where it fell in our conversation – Beckett added a strange remark: 'I'll need some substantive-actors.' An example of a direction that, judging by the tone in which Beckett gave it, was at first glance resistant to interpretation. To ask for an explanation, which never occurred to me in such cases, would have been to ignore the fact that Beckett's rare utterances about what he was looking for were conditioned by the neutrality he observed with regard to himself, and were inseparable from the state of indifference, from that undifferentiated zone, which was precisely where he sought, who knows, through words, what was necessary to maintain this neutrality. It was not that he foreswore all questions in advance; such pride was absolutely foreign to him and hermetism or oracular attitudes seemed pitiful to him. Perhaps Beckett was alluding to the immobility imposed upon the actress playing the Mouth of *Not I* (Billie Whitelaw: he admired her *tour de force*), to the Listener of *That Time*, to the lugubrious masks of *What Where* (in the filmed version). He used to deplore the painful and almost unbearable effects, even when alleviated by all imaginable expedients (headrests, invisible supports, etc.), which such motionlessness could have when it lasted for hours during rehearsals, and would declare his gratitude and admiration for those who accepted such constraints, an altogether radical diminution of their habitual dramatic means ('How lucky I have been with actors!' 7 September 1986). But this curious expression – substantive-actor – also seems to me to reveal a relationship between a character's movement and voice in Beckett's final plays, be they extant or left incomplete.

Sometimes, the voice seems to be to the movement what the noun is to the sentence; the movement is a sentence governed by the voice; the voice is the subject. On occasion, if one considers the actor-movement relationship, the immobile or almost immobile actor is like a substantive forgotten in a big unfinished sentence. At other points, considering only the voice, one could still say that the actor's voice nominalizes the verbless sentence. Ultimately, the movement itself can be understood as the substance of a vocal sentence; the movement is the subject, whether merely conveyed or actually performed, of a sentence that is a voice.

That Time seems to suggest a verbalized movement (the movement is only expressed, by three spatialized voices), as does *Footfalls* (the movement is performed) and ... *but the clouds* (the movement takes place, but the voice is mute and is only *shown* at the end ...); on the other hand, seemingly closer to the apparently more difficult-to-imagine case of a subject-movement are *Come and Go*, *Rockaby* (the movement of the chair being the substantive of the monologue), and *What Where* (the undefined rotation of the interrogations constraining the Voice, tyrannizing Bam the tyrant's circular recitation).

To speak of substantive-actors was, moreover, to throw up a bridge between the increasingly nominal style of all the narrative texts since *How It Is* and the theatre, a bridge across *Bing* and *Lessness*, which are the most advanced attempts at an elliptical syntax. With Beckett there has always been more Democritus, all things considered, than Heraclitus. The words are atoms, nouns, adverbs.

There is a piece of juvenilia by Beckett (*Dream of Fair to Middling Women*, 1932), which introduces atomism into music: 'The music comes to pieces. The notes fly about all over the place, a cyclone of electrons.'[25] This includes a 'Chinese' fable about someone called Lîng-Liûn who, while chopping wood and taking as a model the six notes emitted by a male phoenix and six others emitted by a female phoenix, puts together a dodecaphonic sequence of liû-liû to which he gives names such as the Yellow Bell, the Equable Law, the Bell of the Woods, etc. Each character in the novel in which this fable is inserted (John, Smeraldina-Rina, Syra-Cusa, Belacqua ...) is assigned one of the liû-liû and the plot, from that point onwards, is just a set of musical arrangements: 'If all our characters were like that – liû-liû-minded – we could write a little book that would be purely melodic; think how nice that would be, linear, a lovely Pythagorean chain-chant solo of cause and effect, a one-fingered teleophony that would be a pleasure to hear [...].'[26] This fantasy, a fragment of an unfinished text to which Beckett was none too attached – as little as to some of his poems and to *More Pricks Than Kicks* – which he instantly asked me not to read, summarily conveys the abstract idea of a kind of linearity obtained through discrete elements combined in relations of 'musical' nature. It is not certain that this intention has been lost in the later works: *Bing* and *Lessness* quite clearly share the same thrust. And it seemed to me that he found a faint reminder of this in the arrangements on the table, assembled with concrete materials and a taste for permutations – arrangements of 'packets'. Man is a packet. Enter Watt: 'Mr Hackett was not sure that it was not a parcel, a carpet for example, or a roll of tarpaulin, wrapped up in dark paper and tied about the middle with a cord.'[27] Tied about the middle with a cord? Nothing is less certain. And scraps of canvas flutter about here and there. At any rate, we had our atoms, syncopated words, blocks of movement, slight collisions of the objects or our fingers on the table. We too were like affixed substantives. Few verbs amongst us, few verbs in our lives, such was the fiction that led me to say to him: 'Each in his own life and us in none at all.'

Laconism is a disposition of the mind and the body, an affection not only of language, but of the whole person. There was in Beckett's very appearance something like an undefined mute exclamation. Always verticality, the cliff face, the bird. Immersion in silence could become so deep that when one of us reverted to words he would take care to articulate them slowly, as if the other had become deaf. But along the perpendicular, through light whirlwinds like scattered ash, there was something that soothed, something noble and human, which one really must resolve to call gentleness. It is nothing, perhaps. It is nothing, to be sure, among the many ways one must represent the world to oneself. Perhaps this has no relation to this writer, one writer among so many others, that is not purely contingent and assuredly without significance for his work, or interest for anybody, unless linked to this *ponderación misteriosa* is the event of friendship. So I cling on to it, seeing nothing else for the moment, and I will go on for a bit longer trying to set down, on this faint but unlimited map, the declension of the most modest gestures. Thus proceeds memory, again via substantives, and within each one are found others, piled up, each posthumous to the one that comes after itself, as if 'the familiar phrases, the personal art, the singular souls of the dead' were being preformed in the interlocking words, as if the gestures that fade away were becoming creation in reverse.

There was the packet of little cigars. Beckett would place it on the table, open it, take a cigar, offer me one, then another one. He would smoke one, I would invariably smoke two. On the advice of his doctor, he had cut down his consumption to three or four per day, but he smoked more again towards the end. I saw seven different brands in succession. He would mention rare ones, which I would seek out for him (something I continue to do), without much success. I unearthed one of them in an old-fashioned tobacconist, of the sort everyone likes, in Strasbourg, and then in Basel, where I went to see the carnival I later described to him – the methodical corteges of tropical masks behind the fife-players moving through frozen streets. While getting up, Beckett would point out that I was forgetting the cigars, thinking they belonged to me ('But they are yours! They are yours!'), or else, without a word, by way of goodbye, would flick the packet in my direction. He would only have a coffee, sometimes a large one, on other occasions *un petit noir*, to use the conventional and already dated expression, and me, a whiskey to drown out the ever-possible tension and allow him to feign surprise: 'You're giving yourself up to drink ... in the morning?'

We often happened to talk about substances: ineffective medication, firewood, the quality of wool in overcoats. Then he would incline his head over his cup of coffee, looking at it from an angle, observing the surface, contemplating its reflections. Dreamily, he would plunge the wrapper into the coffee instead of the sugar, would light his cigar at both ends. The convex lenses of his glasses, which replaced, he would say while waving them about, the crystalline of his eyes, were all scratched because he was forever moving them carelessly around the table.

I used to see these details because of the hands. Beckett himself always paid special attention to hands. They are the object of more and more insistent allusions in the final texts, but *How It Is* had already devoted several pages to them. He would have liked to do a play 'about nothing but them' because they are, he would say, 'so photogenic'. He felt for hands a kind of compassion, which I too had felt as a child. 'At rest after all they did', and they are still there for hiding the face in ruins, the head which cannot take any more – an ultimate, fragile barrier. Consider the old woman's hands carrying the flowers on the staircase of *Film*. Nobody made better use of the gesture of shielding one's face than Beckett, nobody better than he turned this humble refusal into something like the last possible signal. In this respect, the final images of *Film* are emblematic, and Beckett had not forgotten Buster Keaton's ever-so-beautiful hands; it was the only good memory he had of that shoot, for the two men, contrary to what one would like to imagine, had not understood each other at all.

His own were big, long, bony, and as if irregular; more ligneous than leaved; certain articulations tyrannized others, several phalanges were seized up, with the ring finger leading an independent existence, imperceptibly wandering about the handle of a cup, or a lighter; the skin, fine and sensitive, prone to the most spectacular bruises; the nails often cracked. The quite fantastically rigidified fingers would struggle against asphyxia. Like the protagonist of *Catastrophe*, Beckett was afflicted by Dupuytren's contracture. Owing to a kind of atrophy, as I understood it, the fingers are left permanently clenched: 'It's like a claw.' Beckett thought, it must be said, about surgical intervention ('You're looking surgical this morning,' he once said, in a huff); then gave up the idea. But he was worried about losing the use of the middle finger, which would have made writing near impossible. It was already a rather acrobatic feat, under these conditions, to produce that spidery calligraphy, which would reliably appear, on stamped envelopes, slid under my rickety door, and rouse me from slumber. Around the age of eighty, he took up the piano again, coaxing his hands to puzzle through several Haydn sonatas – 'exclusively,' he would specify. And he would say: 'Time passes ... it's marvellous ... and it's so beautiful.' I could see Goethe's ghost inclining over him.

When it came to opening a door, the hands seemed to invade his whole body: he would lean in, examining it, then he would apply his palm to a panel and burst forth, immediately straightening up, with his probing step, as if taken aback at having encountered little resistance. Those moments in the distance, when nothing was happening save for an upward movement equal to the disappearance of all possibility of going beyond, were already retreating far into themselves, anticipating the absence that was going to follow the undefined return of the thresholds I am trying to scrutinize here (that, for example, of the shift to the familiar *tu* form, adopted straightaway whenever Beckett used to give me something: 'Here, take this').

Just as his movements would alternate between dips and upturns, Beckett's handwriting varied in length and breadth. It is difficult to give anything other than a general impression to those unfamiliar with graphological descriptions, or who, despite being in the habit of deciphering it, have perhaps missed a certain essential and recurrent trait. I observe that Beckett did not have a single way of writing, but at least five during these ten years, and the little I have seen of older manuscripts leads me to think he used to have more, each one extracted from another, sprung with as much energy as the stiffened hand that set them down retained in lively subtlety. Just as *The Unnameable* gyrates and as each gesture, fluctuating, clothes another even more powerless gesture, so Beckett's script was as finely folded in on itself as the pages that emerged were imposing. He confessed to having occasional difficulty re-reading himself. Minuscule asperities, very fine serrations veering from left to right as if blown by a powerful wind, processions of birds scattered by the crossing over an unstitched page wandering off the coast of the big wavering margins, but ranged in good order like penitents in purgatory: these are some aspects of the private handwriting. The second variety, perhaps the most beautiful, was an artist's proof reserved for friends, in very black ink, *wie gestochen*, as my grandmother, who was twelve years older than Beckett, used to say; she would ask me to pass on her compliments to her own parents and lived so cut off from time that she expressed her astonishment at having heard no more news, from the newspapers, of Blaise Pascal ... This engraver's writing, always closely packed, rising, and heavily sloping – with certain letters more symbolized than traced out and others abridged by those that followed – somewhat recalled

La Fontaine's, judging by an autograph I had seen; I told him this and it pleased him greatly.

A third version, generally in paler ink, marked a return to the looseness of what the Chinese call 'grass script', like a rope abandoned on the shore, with the words very spaced out and so horizontal that you could turn the page around and see Mongolian calligraphy emerging from top to bottom. (Between the fabulist and Genghis Khan, which would you choose? There is a bit of both, there really is a bit of both, you can check.) One variant displayed a much firmer line, nervous, spread out on the page, quite majestic; it is common in the manuscripts from the 1960s. Contrasting with this were: 4°) a compressed script, with almost absent downstrokes, the script of worries and 5°) the official calligraphy, open, diligent, very readable, for use in addresses, thank-you notes, carefully maintained production notebooks, pages copied out for reproduction and publication.

The messages we exchanged used to contain, among other things, information concerning our respective movements; we would regularly keep each other 'up to date', as he liked to put it. Of the three homes at which they were sent to me, the second held particular interest for Beckett. That is why I speak of it here. It was just a bedroom, digs, he would say familiarly, to which, even after moving on, I remained very attached; and he himself advised me to keep it for friends when I decamped elsewhere. Located on the rue de Condé, it was beautiful because it was cube-shaped; poorly whitewashed walls, a rough parquet, two big windows overlooking old façades; sparsely furnished would be an overstatement; without mod cons, without hot water for several years, a chimney the sole decoration. Like the rest of the whole street, or almost all of it, I used wood to keep warm; and, come winter, one of the capital's last wood-sellers would carry out the delivery, house by house; it used to take a whole morning. A robust, silent and busy man hauled the sacks of logs upstairs, unloading his burden among the books, on the floor, where this supply would remain, taking up a good part of the available space, until spring. And so I lived hidden away, two steps away from the clamour of the carrefour de l'Odéon, behind heaps of wood. Across the way lived a reclusive old woman; she used to read all night long. Behind windows opaque with dust, her silhouette would catch a ray of light and pick up a book: so I myself would try and read the variations of her luminescence. In the street, our lamps kept each other company. At dawn, when I turned out my own, hers would still be shining. A hundred times, I was on the verge of paying her a visit without ever following through.

Beckett too used to sit by windows, and there is a beautiful story Elmar Tophoven, his German translator, told me; maybe it is already known, no matter, I repeat it here in memory of our mutual friend, an extraordinary man, whose illness and premature death on 23 April 1989 darkened the last year that Beckett had left to live (what a strange and cruel turn of phrase!). Tophoven, as was his custom for thirty years, was revising a version in Beckett's home with him when suddenly the writer, asking his inter-preter to excuse him, opened a window. The view looked out over La Santé Prison. For some time already, Top had noticed Beckett's distracted state, and then something moving about the walls, like a flickering glimmer. It was the reflection of a mirror. An inmate was sending a signal to the free man opposite, the nondescript man, who, alone, would make sweeping semaphore gestures in return, which signified nothing save for: 'Courage!'

After that, I dare not revert to my wood storeroom, which, I know well, was altogether palatial in comparison with certain dwellings formerly found in Paris and that one perhaps finds still, in spite of the appalling and even unthinkable transformations that city continues to undergo. And I am always amazed that Beckett's creatures appear to us sort of isolated and seemingly archetypical given that, without going all the way back to Ireland and Synge's vagabonds (*The Vagrants of Wicklow*, which opens with the henceforth familiar image of the hundred-year-old tramp with long white hair), Paris in the 1950s was not short of human beings close in dress, wiles, tastes, and in their sense of freedom to Molloy and Malone; evidence for this can be found in a series of beautiful tales published at that time by Denoël (with a grey cover and the title written inside a white oval), among which stands out the amazing trilogy, still assiduously consulted by Paris devotees, of books by Jean-Paul Clébert (*Paris Insolite*), Jacques Yonnet (*Enchantements sur Paris*[28]), and Robert Giraud (*Le Vin des rues*[29]). The first of these is from 1952, the year of *Waiting for Godot* and *Malone Dies*, the very same year Robert Doisneau took his photograph of 'un consommateur'. The polyphonic character of Beckett's genius has perhaps somewhat occluded his realism. Among my very few regrets is not having broached this question (but it was unfeasible), not having at least considered talking to him about publications from this period, which were not deemed part of 'official literature', or did not benefit from the glare of publicity. For it is curious all the same to see how post-war French literature has been subject to a very false projection whereby the indisputable greatness and increasing notoriety of radically innovative writers, who were indeed numerous, have led to a disproportionate narrowing of perspectives and consigned to dignified obscurity certain writers who began around the same time to publish a series of works that included some veritable unknown masterpieces. I praised one of these to Beckett, which was devoted in part to the death of lichen; I had copied out numerous pages that I find absolutely perfect, some of the most beautiful prose one can read today. This was *Le Présage* by Pierre Gascar[30] who wrote many other books that I deeply admire: *Le Meilleur de la vie* (1964), *Les Charmes* (1965), *Les Chimères* (1969), *Les Sources* (1975), etc. Beckett too aspired to make something beautiful and could recognize everywhere those who had attempted this as well as those who, like Pierre Gascar, had succeeded.

Behind the rare expressions of appreciation, there lay the insistent question of the relationship between beauty and horror. We had read Jean Genet's *Quatre heures à Chatila* and I observed how the impassiveness of the account did justice to the atrocity of the deeds carried out, gave the accusation its absolute character and yet there was something troubling about it. 'Yes,' he replied, 'it's the same paradox with Kafka: horror of the content, serenity of the form.' Another regret is not having listened to him one day when he started to bring up Céline. It was shortly after the publication of the second volume, which I had not yet read, of the Pléiade edition of his novels had stirred up some controversy that must have affected me, and Beckett, with his seismographic sensitivity, perceived an infinitesimal flinch on my part and stopped talking.

He feared winter, the 'Winter God' whose rout, as he saw it, Horace proclaimed. We also accorded him a place in our conversations and Beckett would often ask if I kept my place well heated. I told him about the bedroom, the wood, and I even mentioned the lengths of iron wire wrapped around the faggots, which were quite rigid and fastened with a buckle; I was not going to throw them out! I used to hold onto these hoops, slotting one into the other at two points along an imaginary sphere, which they enclosed like dented lines of longitude, fashioning, once the material had been freed up by combustion, a sort of slender, graceful mobile in the shape of a hollow planet, which I would hang on the standard lamp ending in a menacing arrow. This trifling object used to serve nonetheless, come summer, as a landing strip at the disposal of several flies. I had ample opportunity to verify, thanks to the slender surface of these strips and the fairly wide choice they offered the fly due to their number and their relative proximity, that the fly, as Jacob von Uexküll teaches us,[31] indeed navigates in accordance with the practice of coastal navigation, which was a not insignificant announcement to be made to Beckett, who kept himself informed about these nice little experiments while sometimes asking me how I was getting on with my 'cherished studies'.

I had, like Beckett, retained a certain affection for things of no value. Knowing that we agreed on the fact that nothing is too humble for us not to pay attention to it, he would mention barrowfuls of dead leaves, chestnuts gathered in Ussy, carefully piled up and then thrown into the distance one by one with a carefree gesture (he would give a hint of this gesture), or how he had worn himself out ('it shattered me') dismantling, at the edge of the forest (of an expanding forest), a symbolic boundary: about one hundred posts fixed in concrete, along with a kilometre of wire; the difficult part, according to him, had been to find a way of rolling it up. This was in July 1983, he was seventy-seven years old and the task involved problems altogether thornier than my aerodrome building; but we had understood each other:

> *Quod vitae sectabor iter, si plena tumultu*
> *Sunt fora?* [32]

We used to blot out this question by mutual consent, the one which Descartes, in a dream, had seen emerging on a page of Ausonius; each from a very different place; in an opposing direction, but with the same gesture. Tumultus had grown without covering up the resulting silence; it had ever been thus. There is no path, it is understood, save for over very short distances that are always on the verge of plunging into the unmeasured. When occasionally mentioning the fate of such and such a deceased friend, Beckett would never consider him from any point of view that would have summoned a fixed image – a closed face; rather, he would retain an indefinitely open detail, which did not insist on being appreciated in any particular way. He had for that matter said to Top in German: '*Man kann nie genug wissen, aber nicht um zu verurteilen*' ('One can never know enough, but not in order to judge'). In this respect too, fame was without importance. In truth, he found it dreadful, he whispered to me one day in a near-inaudible murmur.

From the threshold of the house where I am recording these memories, far from the Paris we loved, in a Vermont village, I spy with my little eye a van passing by (it's a children's rhyme), that bears this inscription: *Landscaping*.[33] A conversation is a piece of *landscaping*, it draws the outline of a landscape. Many parts of it remain obscure. Ours resided in Paris. Beckett loved Paris. He loved that people walked there, like him. 'Do you always walk as much?' he would ask me in the early days, and the fact of having devoted hours to certain well-defined routes served as a voucher for obtaining his consideration. We used to compare notes. He introduced me to little corners, pointed out myriad details, showing me new ways to weave through the streets.

At that time I was divagating among the sciences; he was indifferent to none of them. His mind had retained an encyclopaedic cast. Only philosophy, in which, although he did not want to admit it, he was well versed, brought forth a certain reticence within him – the shrug of the shoulders of which Adorno speaks. I nonetheless had the joy of suggesting myself as a go-between, asking Jacques

Derrida, one of my lecturers at the École Normale, to allow me to pass on to Beckett his *Ulysse gramophone. Deux mots pour Joyce*.[34] Moreover, Beckett questioned me, on several occasions, about the activities of the two great philosophers I told him I admired above all, Deleuze and Derrida; what especially interested him was the style of their oral teaching, the temperament of their voices and the sense of uplift one would feel while listening to a philosophical voice. I would first describe the concrete conditions under which they spoke, so as to deplore the fact that these had not really been up to their standards, then the perceptible characteristics of the tone particular to each of them, and how I was affected by this: Derrida's inflexible meticulousness suddenly unlocking, after a long analysis driven forward step by step, a dazzling advance whose light would stream majestically over the text being studied, henceforth invested with a definitive boldness; Deleuze's almost melodious structure, choosing with princely ease, from each slowly identified concept, its most beautiful aspect, its overarching pattern, so as to lay them on an immaculate tablecloth that one would discover, stretching as far as the eye could see, which was the exposition of these ideas itself. I would speak of their exquisite courtesy, not without irony and interspersed with bursts of savagery, their unfailing patience, their crazy generosity. Beckett would listen, attentive, nodding his head with an air of profound contentment. I probably did not express myself in those exact terms at the time; what is certain is that he asked me what kind of men these philosophers really were; and I owe it to the truth to repeat the word by which I summed up what I had said: deep down, they were noble (*edle Menschen*). Beckett was satisfied by this response. It was he who had made me develop the habit of continuing to search for the goodness at the heart of the most dazzling talent and mental rigour become musical.

Into this same landscape, I also had the opportunity to introduce a slender fragment of China. In 1986, the Paris Autumn Festival had devoted to China a programme of events without equal. On 4, 8, 9 and 10 October, in the 'tea house' erected in the Palais de Chaillot, I went to see, from the same seat in the second row on the left-hand side, the same marvellous performance. So when Beckett, on 12 October, confronted me with the question that he liked to ask from that point onwards: 'So then, tell me something!' I naturally spoke to him of the Dong. This national minority, one of fifty-five recorded, occupies a mountainous region in central China on the borders of Guizhou, Hunan, and Guangxi.[35] A choir of nine Guizhou women, from the village of Kaili, had just performed, for the first time outside of China and maybe even that province, a kind of music, which, as much as the sight of their arrival on stage, had moved me deeply. Coiffed in headdresses of bouquets of silver flowers, intertwined with one or two real red or yellow blooms, clad in knee-length bronze and purple tunics, blue sleeves with white turn-ups threaded with red, bronze-coloured gaiters tied up with white, sky blue slippers brocaded with silver, earrings, braided necklaces (torcs) culminating in a spiral around the neck, as if locked into place by a strange key, and breastplates of *repoussé* silver on which little bells tinkled away, they would be lined up (in front of the Eiffel Tower all lit up in the background), displaying beautiful foreheads that refracted the singing and on which the exertions of the sinuses could be seen, as well as little seisms of the lips and admirable teeth through which the music flowed. The first impression was of voices projected as if by little girls in unison eager to show that they are very well-behaved. But never has the Homeric expression appeared to me so apt: the barrier of your teeth, Dong woman. That was the instrument, the most instrumentalized part of their bodies, which would trace a straight line at unvarying altitude supported by the plinth of shoulders and hips. This ridgeline would run over a series of long sustained notes, sung in a dissimulated voice, then syllabification would resume – little aerial explosions along an unbreakable thread, stretched like a crystalline sieve, a ligament hooked, to finish off, onto two ascending marches which led to the reply: *Ei zio*, 'over to you, your turn'. For, we were told, as a people they sing all the time, principally in alternated responses, during competitions, when invitations are being exchanged between boys and girls, where 'the voice constitutes the principal means of seduction', and in the course of ceremonies at the 'Drum Tower'; 'but also while working in the fields, when receiving and bidding farewell to guests; some even ask for directions while singing'[36] (had Oedipus sung, had Laius sung along the fatal path, who knows, things would have worked out ...). As for the texture itself of this polyphony, the specialists gave it a rather loose definition; the brochure handed out to the audience said that 'the melody is developed on a tenor bell, or else the voices shift in parallel. This repertoire could, according to certain Chinese musicologists, be at the root of Byzantine music.' Music soaring across ancient empires, voyaging like gods, how could you not applaud it? I yielded all the more willingly given that there was in the choir a very beautiful woman, very pale, with eyes always raised and a highborn face wishing to conceal itself, undoubtedly the face of a Byzantine empress.

The programme conveyed some quite fantastic information about the Dong: 'Their towers and their bridges are the most beautiful in China'; these wooden towers have ten stories, but 'use neither nails nor rivets, the elements are assembled using mortises and tenons'; and then, within these 'tightly knit' and nevertheless 'dispersed' communities, 'having a beautiful voice is the most esteemed gift'. Finally, a self-evident truth. All in all, 'chased towards the mountains', excellent architects, master carpenters, great musicians, the Dong had risen up. I had taken photos, and had even gone as far as exceptionally obtaining a private recording so that I could supply the lot to Beckett. I can still see the old Irishman, like a radio operator in his hutch, with both hands, using all his strength to press the headphones to his ears, shouting at me nonetheless to lower the volume, listening, head bowed, eyes closed, to this extraordinary music that had come from the unknown heart of China. I played him a solo performed on a *pipa* by the woman who, amongst all of them, had seduced me. She was standing in the centre, to the left of the empress. She alone wore two flowers in her hair. Still facing forward, she happened to turn her head and, for an instant, the distance separating us collapsed. It's incredible, I said to myself, hypnotized, the depth begins behind her temples. She was smiling to excuse herself for not being unreal. I was thinking about Michaux: 'Oh first smile of the yellow race. Everything is hard in me and arid, but her smile, so fresh, yet appears to me to be the mirror of myself.' 'Yes, it's very beautiful,' said Beckett. 'Yes, it's very beautiful.' He did not used to say that often ... He granted me that the woman too was extremely beautiful. Then gave a hint of a questioning smile. Of course, I would have strongly wished to pay her my respects, but they kept her very closely guarded. Besides, I speak neither Dong nor Chinese. And yet, on the final day, I eluded the minders and placed between her fine hands, with appropriate silent gestures, a flask of perfume as she was crossing the foyer alone. Beckett, beaming, asked me what brand it was.

In sum, our understanding expressed itself from the outside, through the outside, and the shared moments were all the more precious because they came from far off, unexpected, excentric, exterior to himself. This did not happen without strangeness, for even as we were speaking of everything, sitting outside the centre of his field of vision, I would never stop rereading him, my mind focused on his creatures, but I did not mention it, for I saw in him another man altogether from the one who had inspired them. This is perhaps why it was given to me to understand that he had forgotten them.

People have often wondered what relationship Beckett had maintained with his characters, a relationship whose existence seemed intuitively probable on a level of reality similar to that of second sight, of a perilous crossing, of a river beneath the sea, or even of an inflection. Regardless of any theory, the question is not a naïve one. It arises with the same insistence concerning Dostoyevsky. Cioran, in a passage whose aptness would often resurface in my memory, remarks that one only saw the pattern of filigree in flashes; I also had this impression, without being able to define it other than through these images: weft, outcrop:

> Beings who do not know if they are still alive, in the grip of immense fatigue, [...] all conceived by a man whom one guesses to be vulnerable and who wears out of modesty the mask of invulnerability. I had, not so long ago, in a flash, a vision of the bonds that join them to their author, to their accomplice ... I would be unable to translate what I saw, rather what I felt, at that instant into an intelligible expression. It remains that, ever since, the least of his heroes' remarks reminds me of the inflections of a certain voice [...][37]

It was through forgetting that he drew alongside his own: he had made himself forget about them. Forgetting had become a force within him, attested by the peace in which his creatures left him. He had adopted the most humble disguise; but whoever confused this with the feeling of indifference that writers often have for their completed works would have been blind to what was effusive and profoundly insurrectional about forgetting in Beckett. He would say to me of himself: 'He's become foreign to me, this author. I can't bring myself to believe in it' (20 May 1984), or else, of *The Unnameable*: 'That's become completely foreign to me. I don't know this author' (10 October 1984). And I responded boldly to him: 'I understand you.' He looked at me, surprised: 'You understand me?' – and of course, it was true, I also understood that it was indeed a matter of life, of life damaged in the thunderous murmur that one does not raise twice; it was deeply moving to feel him so distant and yet so close. The hint of a different time would pass between these most simple words, from one bank to the other, and the river would climb back towards its source, immobile.

To converse peacefully, under cover of forgetting – fiction on top of fictions – with the author of terrible dialogues, with him I had dropped the anchor of idleness. Maybe we gave up when it became real. This is also where music used to find its place, at the root of the extinction of sounds. To the question: 'What would you have done if you had not been a writer?' he supposedly responded, I once read, I forget where, that he would have listened to music. Music as idleness, this temptation was close, beyond the distance separating us.

The rare mentions of work in progress, which, in spite of everything, we would happen to discuss, always of his own free will, without any prompting on my part, only became all the more precious for being so infrequent; however, they remained isolated and unsituated. I could not tell him how apt they seemed to me ... How had he advanced, with his light step, along the bridge hanging beyond The Unnameable? I would see old perspectives sliding towards us, it even seemed to me sometimes that everything was getting mixed up and that the music of the work was coming back upon us in silence.

Mercier and Camier, Estragon and Vladimir were still talking to each other. Subsequently the echo chambers, even if they are part of a monologue, become entirely heterogeneous milieux and end up stellar distances apart ('From one world to another, it's as though they drew together,' says, ironically, the Opener of *Cascando* (1963); 'so wan and still and so ravished away that it seems no more of the earth than Mira in the Whale [...]' [*Words and Music* 1962]). Henceforth, the beings hear each other as the light of dead stars reaches us, *the voice become visual*; the pathway has become uncrossable. Words have at last become the element of the disjunction that had already so powerfully governed the ratiocinations of Watt and his evolutions in the house of Mister Knott.

Separated by speech on the easel of silence, Beckett's beings open themselves up less to the being-there than to the being of the problematical.[38] After *Krapp's Last Tape*, the idea of a constitutive disjunction is successively constructed in *Embers* (1959), *Rough for Radio I* (1960-1, published in 1976), *Words and Music*, and *Cascando*. This group of radio plays, seemingly modest and circumstantial, provides a key to understanding the work that Beckett imposes - the performance he gives - upon aporias in which, after *Texts for Nothing* and notwithstanding the dazzling darkness of *Endgame*, it seemed improbable he could remain; yet it is their insistence itself that he raises to the level of schematism, towards which he will go on striving up until the graph of *Quadrat I + II (Quad)* (1982). It is through the miniature forms, the minor genres he creates from scratch, that Beckett reopens the previously abandoned games; it is still true twenty years on, when everything seems to have been said, since the force of detachment invented in the radio pieces from the 1960s forms a field with *Quadrat*. And the *mise en abyme* is as obvious, though limited, in *Rough for Radio I*, as it is generalized, in accordance with the law of genre, in *Ohio Impromptu* (1981). Other connections readily appear: it is clear, for example, that *What Where* (1983) reprises, albeit superimposed onto the plan of another framework constructed in the meantime, the principle that operates in *Cascando*. The small-format works, scattered between 1972 and 1983, are in fact the extremely meticulous pages of a composition whose full extent will only become clear when held against the light, at the edges of the tracings placed one on top of the other. This work remains simple and goes on simplifying itself, as if each surface, once filled in, would then release a purer line.

Valéry's vow: 'Remove everything I see there!' seems be realized within these reduced spaces where the light is concentrated – buoyant and very bright wherries sailing in the general penumbra. There is a kind of gaiety particular to these cruelly scrutinized enclaves, there is a Beckett kind of clarity that is lively and melodious, for (let us paraphrase it in another way), the ear sees, perceives variations of vocal textures, in accordance with lines, paces, and mental trajectories reflected in the space. *Faute de mieux*, it sees diagrams. When these are for the stage, they have to be traced out with the utmost meticulousness; in fact, it is enough to follow them as rigorously as possible, while refraining from interpretation, so as to obtain results of confounding power, given the few elements involved in the operation, whose nature then becomes manifest: it is a *potentialization*. But if the person staging the play refuses to efface himself and accept this discipline, the effect becomes attenuated in proportion to the independence he allots himself; if he makes liberal use of this, as occasionally happened even during the author's life, then he precipitates the play into insignificance. The slightest modification inflicted upon the structure regulating *Footfalls* makes the play lose all interest. The later dramaticules are prone to the worst misadventures: of one extravagant instance, that occurred in 1982, Beckett could only laugh, such had the stupidity masquerading beneath his name been given free rein. Separated from its exact conditions of enactment, Beckett's theatre falls into imagery whereas it is really the achievement of a kind of stasis, like music.

Rejecting an authority that they are, however, not averse to using as a basis for establishing their own, some directors, under the pretext of freedom, hasten to suppress the only kind of freedom holding some interest in this case: the freedom that the work has to do without them. Like any work, Beckett's overlays a power (who could not see that it expresses itself to the full, for example, in Hamm's ferocious voice?), and if it is a question of misery, it is only at the surface of this power, a power of x where x certainly takes on some murky values but also some wild shades among the shreds of the seamless coat. If, from the most indigent burblings of the person reduced to his ultimate and pathetic attributes, you do not bring out the irreducible impersonal incantation, if in the corroded words one does make heard an invisible insistence, an 'eternal harping',[39] 'this not one of us harping harping mad too with weariness to have done with him',[40] what Artaud, for his part, calls 'the psychic foot-stamping of a pattern',[41] something tirelessly rotative, immanent and salvatory in Beckett's work – then better off forgetting about it altogether.

Dismayed by the ever-growing number of deliberate misinterpretations, tempted to give up all interventions, and although he could count on a small group of friends spread around the world – most of them isolated, at the margins of major companies – who stayed in touch with him and worked under his effective direction when circumstances permitted, Beckett clearly knew himself to be rowing henceforth against the tide along which contemporary theatre on the whole was drifting. And, even as regards the past, he saw it as a stroke of luck that he had met people who defended him, Roger Blin, Alan Schneider, to mention only two major interpreters whose deaths, three months apart (1984), affected him greatly. (Beckett's dominant feeling with regard to those who had made his work known was one of gratitude, as touched as it was touching; without them, he used to repeat, nothing would have happened, he would never have been heard, his work was being refused everywhere, he owed them everything ... That this could conceivably have been mutual hardly seemed to cross his mind.)

However, as for his attitude in later years, he remained sceptical concerning his reception, although he knew that he would leave it at that. Of *Worstward Ho* (1983), which he thought it impossible to translate into French ('Even the first word is untranslatable, if not without great sacrifices.' 6 July 1983), he claimed to have heard only a few reactions.

I felt a strange feeling, obviously mixed with sadness, when he told me with simplicity: 'It's the last full stop.' 'I still recognize myself in it,' he added (20 May 1984). One year previously, on 19 May 1983, he was already writing to me: 'I believe that *Worstward Ho* has finished me off.' (In this vein, some notes took an ironic and lugubrious turn: 'Next Sunday 25, such and such a place, such and such a time. My remains will be there.') In sum, like Joyce in a way, he also finished his work abruptly, on a cliff face.[42]

With great simplicity, a distant kinship with the discarded, the locked-away, the simple beings whom he had brought into the light, would shine through (Cioran also brings this up) in his unflagging interest in the elementary dispositions of existence, sleep, music, comings and goings, the aforementioned bedroom, heating, and winter clothes (on the other hand, he kept his counsel about food, illnesses, hospitals). As we used to do with our glasses, we would compare our overcoats: I used to have a very well-worn one, found in the Saint-Ouen flea market years ago, supposedly made of camel-hair (like John the Baptist's tunic), whose fabric he would touch, repeating with an incredulous air: '*Kamelhaar*, camel-hair' (I think that together we were imagining these improbable camels). Then I had another one made, warmer, something he encouraged, in a very heavy blue-black cloth, which he liked a lot; he started trying out other terms on it, like this one for example, as if torn from a dream: 'Alpaga?' Indeed he would, on occasion, suddenly ask me the meaning of a non-existent word.

He always wore the same thing: sometimes a blue reefer jacket with tartan lining, occasionally combined with a fine

71

blue cashmere scarf (you can see this outfit in several of John Minihan's photographs); on other occasions, a sheepskin coat with a wide, fur-lined collar and a curious little brown woolly hat, which Suzanne had also found in Saint-Ouen twenty or thirty years beforehand, that he would pull down to his ears, thus making himself, in a somewhat comic effect, resemble an aviator from Blériot's time. Outside of winter, an old, cigar-scarred, light brown jacket, with frayed buttonholes, but very elegant, worn over a thick knitted jumper (unravelling here and there) with the collar rolled up, blue, beige, or russet-coloured, or a grey or beige shirt, or even a tracksuit top; grey flannel or ecru beige cotton trousers; feet often bare in espadrilles or else in running shoes. A brown reticule made of fine canvas in the morning, a greenish satchel in the afternoon – for strolling – worn snugly over the shoulder, would complete the most watched silhouette on the boulevard Saint-Jacques or the boulevard Blanqui, which several photographers managed to capture, normally unbeknownst to him, for he really had had enough of photos. From the extreme simplicity of his clothing, with its dominant greys, beiges, and blues, and the cheerful note of the espadrilles and the bluish-green soldier's bag, there emanated an impressive elegance, a grace that was truly rare, which came from his size, his gauntness, from a slight stiffness counterbalanced by his curious gait, at once circumspect and quite majestic, comprising at the same time an indefinable ethereal element, the almost mocking air of a beanpole.

With Beckett, forgetting was his rectitude. There is the cliff face and the overhang. He could easily, when you placed one of his books between his hands, consider it with an astonished air, quickly open it at random, read a paragraph and murmur: 'I vaguely remember' (19 December 1980, 'Still'), or go straight to a passage to verify its presence or some other detail. I knew what to expect. As early as the first meeting, his power of forgetting had appeared to me as being similar to a colour. In memory of his creations' amnesia, that of Molloy and Malone – from whom forgetting bursts like a projectile, from Hamm, Krapp, Pim, Mouth, etc. – Beckett would let himself be caught in its beam, when he was resting; but as soon as he got up again, it was so as to retrieve from outside (or from the loyal shadows, if you like, of tenacious memory), no characters anymore, fewer and fewer characters, but always spaces, space-characters to place in this enigmatic clarity without known source emanating from all around, cylinders, cones, rotundas, and then affects for pervading them with flashes of light and moments of stasis, a *habitus* of whiteness in which repetition hollowed out intervals; as if Beckett had ended up giving a spatial cast to forgetting, a particular volume and curvature, a solid content at last, compact and yet ludic, concretized like a world, but light – like forgetting.

It is true, to judge by the power it imprints on every trait that passes over it, that a work may be coextensive with a plan, with tectonic overthrusts of plans whose faults, block by block, line the surface; but you can also say that it is only hanging by a thread. You pull it towards you, and it's a whole other world that you bring back. Great birds turn in the sky and cut across each other's tilted flight. So I was not particularly surprised to find ourselves alongside Kleist of whom Beckett said he knew almost nothing except for *On the Marionette Theatre*, which he admired. However, from September to December 1983, in the evenings, he read, in German, a work on Kleist that he called boring and interminable, with an attentiveness that left its mark on the slim volume he passed on to me, in place of the expected doorstopper, when he had finished it; the page about the marionettes, for example, is crumpled and dog-eared. But long beforehand (5 July 1982), he had told me of his conviction that one of his dramaticules should in fact be performed in a marionette theatre. It will seem paradoxical that it should have been *Catastrophe* (1982) that prompted this remark, a play dedicated to Václav Havel, in prison at the time, seemingly the most expressly political of all those, beginning with *Waiting for Godot*, where a persecutor holds sway – *Rough for Theatre II*, *Rough for Radio II*, *Cascando*, *Words and Music*, *Play*, *Eh Joe*, *What Where* – a play which, moreover, resolutely emphasizes the theme of the individual's resistance against his annihilation and which concludes with an upended catastrophe, undoubtedly a kind of sombre, stoic, and miraculous victory.

That the gyratory movement and the catatonic paralysis of Beckett's creatures, or their obstinate persistence in clinging on, has always enveloped, or duplicated, a penal environment subject to totalitarian surveillance; that the paradigm of inaccessibly juxtaposed voices, the infinite parallelism of bodies in their cruel reciprocal affections, the tyranny of the light frisking the words without ever extracting the right one or tearing off the last one, that this whole contemporary Passion takes on, in Beckett's work, the recognizable form of a Nazi-style interrogation ('nadzis', as Sam continued to say) or one carried out by the other torturers who epitomize the age, but with the considerable nuance that there is no more hope for them than for their victim (like an incongruous Stoic sage, dispossessed of what he never had and already beyond himself), all this is constant and, having made no little contribution to Beckett's reception in the world, does not call out for any commentary that has not already been formulated. But the force of Beckett's stylization always survived this imprisonment while accentuating its indisputable obviousness. As soon, exceptionally, as a way out bends itself into what is being expressed, be it circular, or even abyssal in turn (as in ... *but the clouds* (1976), *Ohio Impromptu*, *Nacht und Träume*, *Catastrophe*, and *What Where* [1981–3]), the stylization of the expressible must become almost absolute: whence the marionettes, whence the diagrams; whence, finally, this mysterious white voice, which Beckett, he told me on 12 November 1981, regarded as an ultimate objective.

One observes a phenomenon that maintains, who knows, strange relations with what one calls old age: iteration immediately becomes the work: the square and its diagonals (*Quadrat*), the permutation of the tormentors (*What Where*). The concern for containing, through an impersonal and regulated execution, the flood of meaning this iteration never fails to produce, would justify the recourse to marionettes, which Beckett raised as a possibility. Or perhaps it is that pathetic burst of light in *Catastrophe* that made him consider this, although in that case it would have been necessary to abandon the human glance at the end, which affirms the intention of the play. A marionette slowly raising its head to stare at the audience, amid the gradual fading of applause – that too is conceivable; imagination dead imagine, the programme has not changed. Whatever the case may be, it strikes me as interesting to see Beckett looking to thwart himself. For it must be added that he was not happy with the title: the term 'catastrophe' must only be understood in its original sense, the technical sense that it has in Greek tragedy: reversal, turnaround, dénouement of the action, the exact sense that it doubly assumes in the text, but from which Beckett would have liked the ideas implied by the everyday use of the word to be disassociated. In vain did we search for another, more satisfying one.

The faces of *What Where* float in a kind of weightlessness and already, the Listener of *That Time* seemed to be hanging by a thread 'about 10 feet above stage level mid stage off centre'; the *anti-gravity* of marionettes, as Kleist reveals it, is attained in immobility by certain Beckettian persons. The miraculous agility then depends straightaway on the voice alone, on its most characteristic lability (the lips of *Not I*); the voice exuded by the rigid figurine, the voice that takes on the mask of the *persona*, the mummy propelled into space, substitutes itself for the movement of the lines along which the puppet's centre of gravity would travel in Kleist's story. What Kleist said of that line thus applies here to the voice: 'In certain respects, it is something very mysterious.' A voice stripped of its timbre, a voice that peels away, heard beyond extinction, whence rise the stationary waves of logos: broken up by minuscule flashes – miraculous disconnections of an all-the-more implacable continuity. In this regard, Beckett is perhaps strangely close to Michaux.

Each in his own way welcomes the unappeasable: Michaux, with eyes closed, and Beckett, with his ear. He used to work on a purely acoustic basis: 'I have always written for a voice ... *Krapp's Last Tape* was written for the voice of an actor whom I did not know, heard on the radio ...' (5 July 1982). What is singular, irreducibly singular, but tirelessly filtered ... And if, for Kleist, there is only the equally absolute consciousness and unconsciousness that have the potential for grace, a spectral and yet incarnate voice takes on, in Beckett's work, the infinite insistence of the expressible.

Only the shadow emerging from the depths can still make the darkness recede, the shadow that shrouds the rubble of what had been human language. 'It would be necessary to find a *vocal shadow,*' Beckett told me on 12 November 1981, 'a voice that is a shadow. A white voice.' For the shadow in the voice rises up like a spot of clarity when darkness spreads on the stage, a pale and frozen breath, almost inaudible, close, too close, an inflexibly foreign dawn, *and yet it is a murmur of bliss.* 'There remains a world to discover,' he had added. Kleist also used to speak of a world: '*Und hier sei der Punkt, wo die beiden Enden der Ringförmigen Welt ineinandergriffen ...*'[43] *Coincidentia oppositorum, Quadrat,* 'yes, that's it, a static fugue': the perpetual movement of an unceasing interruption and, said Beckett, 'in the centre there is an abyss ...'

'I have always written for a voice': beauty of the outside, beauty of his work between this voice and him, of this voice rejoining itself outside, in the cold and the night imagined for it; a most simple confession and a powerful shortcut. His concision had the attractive force of a magnet. He would listen: one would hear, distinctly, sentences, things, tipping into the emptiness. He was full of ultra-short witty remarks. He would laugh freely, but with a silent laughter. With a kind of immobile clarity, his eyes would also laugh, diaphanous. To his marvellously sceptical look, on 12 April 1986, I responded with a sentence of Pascal's: 'The humility of one creates the pride of many.' He smiled. 'This one, from Jules Renard, is not bad either: *I envy the glory of not being known.*'

He almost got there, when he moved out of his home. I did not visit him at all: he had spoken to me, not long beforehand, of his apprehension at being seen in a defenceless state. He continued to write to me and started to telephone regularly. He asked for news of Top, hospitalized in Germany, whom he could not contact from his own sick bed. In February 1989 both friends called me almost simultaneously, each to inquire about the other. I felt such a shock that Beckett detected it in my breathing. I gave him the reason, as I had once told him of my heartfelt sense that we would have been friends even if he had not written a single word – in a broken voice, probably. A little later, alas, he asked me to come up with a gesture in his name at Elmar's funeral: 'You'll find something.' His last letter evokes this gesture.

That, apparently, is how the story ends, with a gesture dreamt up for the death of a friend. In the vicinity of death's door, friendship remained, unconditional and without end: that letter, I know well, expresses it strongly; as did the previous ones, for that matter. In the most laconic of his notes, shortly before his hospitalization, on a page torn off in haste as if from one of Lichtenberg's notebooks, he replaces the word 'day' with an exclamation mark.

The days, perhaps, are no more: but I shall have seen the eyes, the hands, the wrinkles of a messenger, and yes, I shall dare to say it: of an angel. I have seen the collapsed bridge in the fog, 'no matter how no matter where. Time and grief and self so-called. Oh all to end.'[44] He will have crossed over the broken bridge and the world, of course, will end.

A walkway in the 14th in the middle of the avenue René Coty. It was close to Beckett's apartment and near to the rue Rémy Dumoncel, location of the nursing home where he spent some months before his death from respiratory failure on 22 December 1989. He was buried in Montparnasse Cemetery. (John Minihan, Paris 2005)

NOTES

1. Translator's note: In scholastic philosophy, the habit of glory (*habitus gloriae*) is the quality of being able to freely contemplate the divine essence. According to Thomas Aquinas, this pertains only to the humanity of Christ and to beatified souls in heaven. See Antoine Lévy, *Le Créé et l'incréé. Maxime le confesseur et Thomas d'Aquin. Aux sources de la querelle palamienne*, Paris: J. Vrin, 2006, p. 276.

2. *'Lass uns menschlich sein'*, 'Let us be human'. To this isolated note in Wittgenstein's *Culture and Value*, *The Unnameable* responds with a diagnosis: 'I alone am man and all the rest divine.' Beckett told me that he had never heard anyone talk about Wittgenstein in Dublin: 'Nobody knew him. I'll find out about it.' (20 May 1984).

3. *de pied ferme/ tout en n'attendant plus/ il se passe devant/ allant sans but* ('Mirlitonnades' in *Poèmes suivis de mirlitonnades*, Paris: Éditions de Minuit, 1978). Translator's own translation.

4. Samuel Beckett, *Disjecta, Miscellaneous Writings and a Dramatic Fragment*, by Samuel Beckett, edited with a foreword by Ruby Cohn, London: John Calder, 1983, p. 49. Cf. *'Cupio dissolvi*. Note sur Beckett musicien', *Détail*, no. 3/4, 1991, Atelier cosmopolite de la Fondation Royaumont.

5. *Krapp's Last Tape* in *Samuel Beckett. The Grove Centenary Edition,* ed. Paul Auster, New York: Grove Press, vol. III, *Dramatic Works*, 2006, p. 227.

6. *Krapp's Last Tape, op. cit.*, pp. 226–7.

7. Werner Kaegi, *Jacob Burckhardt. Eine Biographie*, Basel-Stuttgart: Schwabe and Co. Verlag, vol. V, 1973, p. 24: *'Keine dialektische Entwicklung, sondern Explosionen'*.

8. Bitter winter melts away with the welcome change of a spring breeze.

9. *What Where* in *Samuel Beckett. The Grove Centenary Edition,* vol. III, *Dramatic Works, op. cit.*, p. 504.

10. In English in the original.

11. *Cascando* in *Samuel Beckett. The Grove Centenary Edition,* vol. III, *Dramatic Works, op. cit.*, p. 343.

12. In English in the original.

13. Descartes, *Œuvres philosophiques*, ed. F. Alquié, Paris: Garnier, vol. III, 1963, p. 741.

14. According to Georges Canguilhem, if I am not mistaken.

15. Our mind reels, and totters everywhere,/ And is so very constant in its own inconstancy.

16. That winter (1986–7), he was reading William M. Murphy's impressive work, *Prodigal Father. The Life of John Butler Yeats (1839–1922)*, Ithaca: Cornell University Press, 1978.

17. *Watt* in *Samuel Beckett. The Grove Centenary Edition,* vol. I, *Novels, op. cit.*, p. 202.

18. 'not the blue the others at the back' (*How It Is* in *Samuel Beckett. The Grove Centenary Edition,* vol. II, *Novels, op. cit.*, p. 412).

19. *Endgame* in *Samuel Beckett. The Grove Centenary Edition,* vol. III, *Dramatic Works, op. cit.*, p. 150.

20. D 827, op. 43, no. 2, text by Matthäus Casimir von Collin.

21. Holy night, you sinketh down;/ Down also floweth dreams,/ Like your moonlight through space,/ Through the still breast of Men./ They listen with delight;/ And call out, when the day awakes:/ Turn back, oh holy night!/ Fair dreams, turn back!

22. See *The Unnameable*: 'Perhaps it's dawn, evening of night' (*Samuel Beckett. The Grove Centenary Edition,* vol. II, *Novels, op. cit.*, p. 377). Translator's note: The phrase in the main body of the text is originally referenced as a quotation from *Texts for Nothing*. However, this phrase does not appear in the text. It may have been prompted by the following passage: 'This evening, it's always evening, always spoken of as evening,

even when it's morning, it's to make me think night is at hand, bringer of rest.' (*Texts for Nothing* in *Samuel Beckett. The Grove Centenary Edition,* vol. IV, *Poems, Short Fiction, Criticism, op. cit.,* p. 311).

23. *Nuit qui fais tant/ Implorer l'aube/ Nuit de grâce/ Tombe. Poèmes suivis de mirlitonnades, op. cit.,* p. 37. Translator's own translation.

24. Kleist whose *Penthesilea* provided the opportunity for a pantomime in Berlin in 1811. Édith Clever, conducted by H.J. Syberberg, gave a very beautiful mimed declamation of this play on 11 November 1988 at the Théâtre des Bouffes du Nord in Paris, which remains associated in my memory, in terms of perfection, with the performance of *Solo* by David Warrilow at Saint-Denis' Théâtre Gérard-Philipe in 1983.

25. *Disjecta, op. cit.,* p. 45.

26. *Ibid.,* p. 43.

27. *Watt* in *Samuel Beckett. The Grove Centenary Edition,* vol. I, *Novels, op. cit.,* pp. 179–80.

28. Paris: Denoël, 1954. Republished under the title *Rue des Maléfices,* Paris: Phébus, 1987.

29. First published by Seghers, Paris 1949, with photographs by Doisneau, then by Denoël, 1955.

30. *Le Présage,* Paris: Gallimard, 1972 (Prix Goncourt 1953 for *Les Bêtes,* followed by *Le Temps des morts*). I thank Yves Sansonnens for having made me read this work.

31. Jacob von Uexküll, *Mondes animaux et monde humain,* Bibliothèque médiations, Paris: Denoël, 1984.

32. Which path shall I pursue through life, if all ways are beset by uproar?

33. In English in the original.

34. Paris: Galilée, 1987.

35. On this subject, I was only able to consult the work *Ethnies minoritaires chinoises,* Beijing: La Chine en construction, vol. I, 1984.

36. *Ibid.*, p. 209.

37. Cioran, *Exercices d'admiration*, Paris: Gallimard, 1986, p. 105.

38. Although Beckett is not mentioned, chapter 17 of Gilles Deleuze's *Logique du sens*, Paris: Éditions de Minuit, 1969 ('De la genèse statique logique') has always seemed to me to shed a very strong light on this aspect of Beckett's implicit philosophical position.

39. Maurice Blanchot.

40. *How It Is* in *Samuel Beckett. The Grove Centenary Edition, vol. II, Novels, op. cit.*, p. 518.

41. *Œuvres complètes*, Paris: Gallimard, vol. XV, 1981, p. 16.

42. Gide said: 'The finest audacity is that of the end of life. I admire it in Joyce as I have admired it in Mallarmé, in Beethoven, and in some very rare artists, whose work completes itself with a cliff and who present the future with the steepest face of their genius [...]' (Quoted in translation in Richard Ellmann, *James Joyce*, Oxford University Press, 1982, p. 530.)

43. And here is the point where the two ends of the circular world intertwined ...

44. In English in the original.